BEFORE

NICOLA MARSH

Good girl. Bad boy. A world of trouble…

Good girls finish last? Screw that.
Being a small town girl isn't so bad. Unless Mom's the town joke and I've spent my entire life shying away from her flamboyance. College in Las Vegas should be so much cooler. But it's not. Bad things happen. Real bad. So when my brother Reid offers me an all-expenses paid vacation to Australia for a month, I am so there. Discounting the deadly snakes on the outback cattle station, I should be safe. Until I meet Jack.
Jack defines bad boy and then some. He's big, buffed, bronzed, and hotter than any guy I've ever met. His sexy Aussie accent makes me melt. And the guy can cook.
But he's my brother's new bestie and he lives on the other side of the world. There's no future for us.
Is there?

FURTHER READING

Discover other titles by USA TODAY bestselling & multi-award winning author Nicola Marsh at http://www.nicolamarsh.com

More titles by Nicola Marsh in this series:

Brash
Blush
Bold
Bad

Nicola Marsh

Copyright © Nicola Marsh 2013
Published by Nicola Marsh 2013

All the characters in this book have no existence outside the imagination of the author and have no relation whatsoever to anyone bearing the same name or names. They're not distantly inspired by any individual known or unknown to the author and all the incidents in the book are pure invention.

All rights reserved including the right of reproduction in any form. The text or any part of the publication may not be reproduced or transmitted in any form without the written permission of the publisher.

The author acknowledges the copyrighted or trademarked status and trademark owners of the word marks mentioned in this work of fiction.

AUTHOR NOTE

*In this story, Jack McVeigh is Australian.
Here's clarification of the 'Aussie-isms' Jack uses:*

Beer goggles – bleary eyed from being drunk
Get pissed – drunk
Shag – have sex with
Arse – ass
Ute – Utility
Shithouse – bad/useless
Crapper – toilet
Root – have sex with
Swag – bedroll
Spuds – potatoes
Pav – pavlova (meringue based, cream filled dessert)
Mum – Mom
Keep your snake in the cage – keep your dick in your pants
Missus – boss lady
Half-arsed – average

Shot through – leave, abandon
Billabong – a stagnant pool of water
Soft drink – soda
Akubra – iconic felt Australian stockman/cowboy hat

1

JESS

College was overrated. Seriously.

The dorm-hopping, frat-partying, alcohol-imbibing rumors were true. The part where I became a party animal, made a zillion BFFs and took UNLV by storm? Hadn't kicked in yet. I sucked as badly as a freshman at the University of Nevada, Las Vegas, as I had as a student at Hell High, my nickname for my old high school in Craye Canyon. Apparently once a geek, always a geek.

In two semesters I'd attended three frat parties, had drunk two vodkas, one rum and a watered down Long Island Iced Tea. And the only other bed I'd graced besides my own belonged to my roommate's dog, illegally smuggled in whenever she could. Yeah, chalk up permanent virginity status alongside geek. Embarrassing.

On the upside, I didn't live at home any more. One of the

major incentives for busting my ass at high school to enroll at UNLV was the distance. UNVL was over an hour away from my hometown so I'd have to live on campus. Craye Canyon wasn't big enough for Mom and me.

Pity my foray into freedom hadn't lived up to expectations. I'd hoped to shed my good-girl image at college. Yet here I was, last day before summer break, still hanging out in the library. Worse? Still a virgin.

"Hey Jess, you're coming tonight, yeah?"

I glanced across at Dave, my study partner, and bit back my first response of 'I wish.' Somehow, I didn't think the serious bookworm would appreciate the innuendo.

"Think I'll give it a miss," I said, packing my satchel for the last time this semester.

I was free for the summer. Without plans. I couldn't head home, not with Mom in wedding planner frenzy mode. Summer was the busiest month for Nevada weddings and it seemed like every bridezilla in the state wanted Pam Harper to organize their wedding. Poor suckers.

"School's out, Geekette." Dave tweaked my nose. "Time to par-tay."

"That settles it." I elbowed him away. "No way am I going anywhere with a dork who says *par-tay*."

"Now you're just playing hard to get." Dave slung an arm across my shoulder, a friendly gesture I'd tolerated during our many study sessions together.

"Yeah, that's me, a regular babe juggling guys along with assignments." I rolled my eyes. "Besides, I've got plans tonight."

"What plans?" He snapped his fingers. "Quick, the truth, before you make up some crap."

"I haven't seen my cousin in a while, thought I'd hang out with her."

Truth was, my cousin Chantal worked nights as a dancer at the coolest burlesque venue on the Strip. But she had a great apartment I could hide out in to avoid the inevitable end of semester parties.

I didn't feel like getting drunk, stoned or laid. Not that I'd ever done any of those things before. That Geekette nickname Dave had bestowed on me last August when we both started our undergrad English major? Pathetically true.

"Come to the party with me for a while, then go hang with your cousin later."

When I opened my mouth to protest again, Dave pressed his finger against my lips. "Not talking no for an answer, got it?"

I didn't mind Dave's arm around my shoulder but having his finger against my mouth made me uncomfortable. We were friends. We hung out. Two loners who studied and grabbed the occasional meal. I wasn't remotely attracted to the six foot, reed-thin Mr. Average and I'd never picked up any vibes off him.

But there was something about the way he was looking at me, the way he was muscling in on my personal space, that had me edging away.

"I might see you there," I said, slinging my bag over my shoulder and accidentally on purpose bumping him out of the way in the process.

For a second I thought I glimpsed anger in his pale grey eyes before he blinked and I attributed it to the sunlight filtering through the library windows.

"Okay, catch you later."

I waited until Dave left, watching him lope between the tables and out the main library doors. I liked his easy-going nature, how he joked around without crossing the line. He'd never put the moves on me so the whole touchy-feely finger on the lips? Probably harmless and just me over-reacting to having a long, hot summer stretching ahead of me with not one freaking thing to do.

I needed to get a life.

Fast.

2

JACK

I was a man on a mission.

I needed a bourbon in one hand and a blonde in the other, not necessarily in that order. And the annual Onakie B&S Ball happily provided both.

I'd traveled a long, dusty three hundred miles to attend the black tie Bachelor and Spinster ball in outback Queensland, along with ten thousand other revelers currently jammed into the arena.

Festivities—translated: consuming as much alcohol as humanly possible—had kicked off in the afternoon, gates to the ball opened at seven, which meant there were a lot of B&S's paired off already. Nothing like beer goggles for making a member of the opposite sex appear overly attractive.

I hadn't run into anyone I knew, which suited me just fine. No one from the Cooweer Homestead cattle station where I worked had made the long trek. Then again, considering I was the only twenty-year-old on the property, with the next youngest employee being forty-five, it didn't surprise me. Besides, I preferred it this way. A few hours out of my mundane life to cut free. Go wild. Get pissed. Shag some willing and able chick.

It may not be much, but after spending the last four months working my arse off at the cattle station as a cook, I needed to burn off a little steam.

"Hey handsome. Gotta light?" A thirty-something blonde with sun-wrinkles ringing her big blue eyes touched my forearm, waving a cigarette in her other hand at me.

I shook my head. "Sorry. Don't smoke."

"Too bad." She flung the cigarette away and stepped in closer. "Fancy a drink instead?"

"Got one, thanks." I raised my bourbon. "But don't let me stop you."

Not deterred by my offhand responses, she threaded her fingers through mine. "Let's go dance." She paused and sent me a loaded glance from beneath her lash extensions. "Down by the river."

Code for 'my Ute is parked at the farthest corner of the compound so we can fuck our brains out and no one will hear.'

This is exactly what I'd wanted. A no-strings-attached quickie to alleviate the boredom. So why did the thought of having meaningless sex with a stranger suddenly sound so unappealing?

She stood on her tiptoes and whispered in my ear. "I give great head."

I wasn't too keen, but my cock wasn't so discerning. It stood to attention, straining to get at the brazen blonde.

Sensing my indecision, she tugged on my hand. "Come on."

Like any weak-minded guy who allowed the wrong head to dictate his actions, I fell into step beside her. We dodged a crammed dance floor where an international rock band blasted hard core. We pushed our way through wall-to-wall revelers drunk on booze and each other. We wound our way through Utes and 4WDs parked helter-skelter. We sidestepped couples writhing against each other in the dark.

It was nothing I hadn't seen before. In fact, in the four years since I'd run from the last foster home in Sydney and worked my away across the outback to far north Queensland, I'd attended several B&S balls like this. Lonely people from all walks of life hooking up for a night of raucous fun, endless drinking and faceless sex.

I was over it.

"Here we are." She paused at the last Ute in a haphazard row. I couldn't see its color in the dark but it had an impressive chrome bull bar that shimmered in the moonlight. "You up for it?"

Before I could respond, she had her hand on my cock and her mouth on mine.

I wanted sex. Looked like I was about to get it.

Her tongue dueled with mine, demanding and taunting, as she unzipped me.

I groaned when her hand wrapped around my cock and pulled me free. She squeezed and pulled, teasing me, before dropping to her knees.

The moment her mouth closed around my cock, I closed my eyes, savoring the suction. Just the right amount. No teeth. A skillful gliding action of her mouth that milked me in wet velvet.

She was right. She gave frigging great head.

My balls tightened in anticipation but she was good at this, because she knew the right moment to stop sucking, fish a foil packet out of her bra and roll a condom on me in the time it took for my lust-hazed brain to clear.

"Very nice." She licked her lips with a slow, deliberate sweep of her tongue, before pushing me backward so I was lying flat on my back on the tray of her Ute. "Bet you feel as good as you taste."

She hoisted up her black satin gown and straddled me, giving me a nice eyeful of Brazilian, which she proceeded to play with. Her finger circled her clit as she sank down on me with a moan that raised the hairs on my arms.

There was something incredibly sexy about an uninhibited older woman bouncing up and down on the end of my cock, so into it that I was nothing but an adjunct to her pleasure.

It didn't take long for either of us. She brought herself to orgasm as she slammed down on me at a frantic pace, impaling herself so hard I saw stars when I came. Though that could've literally been the stars clustered in the clear outback sky framed behind her.

"How old are you?" she said as she clambered off and headed around the side of the Ute to the cabin, giving me time to take care of the condom and zip up.

"Twenty."

She glanced up from the side mirror where she was busy reapplying a vivid red lip-gloss. "That's great. I've always wanted to fuck a guy half my age."

She beamed like I'd just presented her with the best gift ever, while my gut twisted. Guess I was as good at judging women's ages as I was at making decisions about where my life was headed. Absolutely shithouse.

Was this really what I wanted? Working my arse off

cooking for a bunch of non-appreciative pricks for months on end, then spending my down time screwing old chicks?

My life was officially down the crapper.

"Thanks," she said, patting my cheek. "I'm heading back to the ball. See you round."

Not if I could help it and it wasn't until she disappeared from view that I realized we hadn't even exchanged names.

Fuck.

There had to be more to life than this.

3

JESS

I had no idea what I was doing here.

An end of semester party at some college kid's open house a block from the Strip.

Actually, that's a lie. I did know what I was doing here. I just didn't like my motivation.

I wanted to cut loose tonight. Do something completely out of character.

Make out with a stranger? Let some hot guy feel me up? Whatever I wanted, I couldn't describe it exactly, but I wanted more than *this*. This constant edginess that I was missing out on something.

Everyone around me constantly talked about sex. How many times they'd done it. How many guys were useless at finding a clit. How freaking awesome having a guy go down on you was.

I was clueless. I seriously had no idea what any of it

"Maybe I missed you too much?" I winked and the sixty-something cook blushed.

"You're full of it," she said, grabbing a ladle and stirring the stew. "So what really happened?"

I couldn't tell her the truth, for the simple fact I hadn't quite figured out what had happened myself.

After the forty-year-old blonde had rooted me on her Ute, I'd made my way back to the main arena. And stood on the outskirts for the next two hours, feeling like crap.

Empty on the inside. Mixed with a healthy dose of disgust.

What kind of a soulless prick hooked up with nameless women?

Pricks like me.

Because that's how I'd felt, watching couples dance and make out and drink until they were comatose...like I had no soul.

I felt dead on the inside. Like nothing or no one could touch me.

And it had scared the shit out of me.

I'd stopped drinking right then and grabbed a few hours sleep to give the alcohol time to work out of my system, before hitting the road and heading back here.

But the empty feeling hadn't subsided and nothing I did these days could shake it. Not even long rides on horseback, sleeping in a swag beneath the stars or losing myself in concocting new recipes.

I needed to shake things up but had no frigging idea how to do it.

"Nothing happened." I took the chopping board over to the pot and scooped the onions in. "Do we put the spuds in now or later?"

"Stop trying to distract me with cooking talk." She

waggled her finger. "You haven't been yourself since you got back from that ball and I'm worried."

A little piece of my hardened heart melted. Ever since I'd arrived at Cooweer four months ago, Mrs. Gee had been like a makeshift mum. Rather nice, considering I hadn't had a mum since mine had done a runner when I was six. At least she'd lasted two years longer than my dad, who'd bolted when I was four.

Mrs. Gee saved me the choicest cuts of meat, made my favorite passion-fruit pav regularly and imparted her best recipes with regularity. She was great. But I wasn't used to having anyone worry about me, least of all an older woman I barely knew.

"Don't worry about me." I blew her a kiss. "You'd be better off being concerned about me figuring out your secret ingredients and winning the Royal Agricultural Show next year."

She snorted. "You're going to hang around that long?"

I shrugged. "Maybe."

The truth was, I had no idea how long I planned on staying. After Mum left, I spent ten years of my life being shunted from one foster home to another, until I'd had a gutful at sixteen and escaped. Barely. The beating I'd received from a sadistic older 'brother' at that last house stayed with me, all the incentive I needed to fall off the foster system map and go bush. And I'd been traveling ever since, working my way across outback New South Wales and into Queensland.

I liked being a nomad. Multi-tasking; anything from shearing sheep to picking up horseshit. Landing the cooking gig had been totally unexpected and the first thing in my life I actually enjoyed.

"I'll make you a deal." Mrs. Gee folded her arms and

propped against the island bench in the middle of the huge kitchen. "You stick around a little longer and I'll show you how to make my famous jelly lamingtons."

"I don't do cakes," I said, secretly thrilled she liked having me around that much.

"You shove them down that big mouth of yours just fine." She grinned and I smiled back, enjoying our unexpected camaraderie. I didn't let many people get close. Mrs. Gee was definitely an exception to the rule.

"Well, you'll have to stick around another month at least, because we're having house guests." She jerked a thumb over her shoulder at the door leading into the main homestead. "Yanks, apparently. Some politician who works for the missus's father in LA. And his girlfriend."

"So? What's that got to do with me?" I cooked for the station workers, Mrs. Gee handled the homestead. We coexisted in the kitchen in culinary harmony, but I'd be lying if I didn't admit to wanting to cook more than the requisite stews and bolognaise and schnitzels the workers preferred.

"I was thinking..." Surprisingly, she hesitated. Mrs. Gee was never lost for words.

"Don't strain yourself." I deadpanned and she laughed.

"What I was trying to say, smart arse, was I'm thinking you might want to try your hand at some new recipes? Help me out?"

Touched by her offer, I said, "Why?"

She glanced away, her gaze glistening with the sheen of telltale tears. "Because my daughter's having woman's problems in Cairns and I may need to go see her on short notice."

Not wanting to precipitate tears, or hear more about the delicate workings of the female anatomy that Mrs. Gee would gladly impart if I showed the slightest interest, I focused on her offer. "Sorry to hear about your girl, but you want *me* to be in charge of all the cooking if you go?"

I didn't add, *are you insane?*

What did I know about serving the posh food homestead guests regularly expected?

"You can handle it." She opened a nearby cupboard, pulled out a stack of cookbooks and slid them across the bench. "Here. I've made notes on all my favorites, but I reckon you could choose a few of your own and have a go."

"But—"

"There are no guests coming bar the Yanks, so it won't be too difficult." Her eyes crinkled with amusement. "Besides, if it gets too much for you, just serve them bangers and mash."

Somehow, I couldn't see an American politician considering sausages and mashed potatoes gourmet fare.

"You're serious about this?"

She nodded. "I have full confidence in you." She tapped her watch face. "You start shadowing me first thing in the morning."

I'd wanted to shake my life up a little.

Looked like I'd got my wish.

Most guys my age were busy getting a tertiary education, getting a car and getting laid.

Me? I had nothing but a spatula in one hand and a stack of cookbooks in another. Not quite the excitement I craved but hey, a guy had to start somewhere.

5

JESS

"Drink this." Chantal thrust a brandy at me. "It'll settle your nerves."

"I'm not nervous, I'm freaking furious." I took the drink and downed it in three gulps, coughing and spluttering as it burned my throat.

"That's why you should agree to my plan." Chantal made a scissor action with her fingers. "Castration is the only answer for slimy bastards like that."

"I'm actually angry at myself."

And I was. Downright livid, that I'd put myself in the position to be raped. I should've been more tuned to the vibes Dave had been giving off, should've been more savvy than to enter a bedroom, albeit with a friend.

Mom always said I was too naive. Having to admit she was right stung almost as much as me misjudging Dave.

"You did nothing wrong," Chantal said, curling up on the sofa next to me. "Don't blame yourself."

"That's the thing. I do." My voice came out soft and pathetically needy. "I'm clueless when it comes to guys."

"How so?" Chantal glanced away, like she couldn't look me in the eye and lie. Because the fact was, we'd both grown up in Craye Canyon. Small town life with a small town mentality. I'd been a goody-two-shoes, trying my best to be the opposite of Mom. Chantal knew this. She'd teased me about it.

Lucky for my brazen cousin, she'd never cared what anyone thought of her and had fled town as soon as she turned eighteen. Now, four years later, here we both were. One of us was a stunning blonde dancer who enticed men for a living. The other one was a dweeby, good girl who hadn't got to first base with a guy.

"I don't flirt, I don't date, I don't have any freaking idea when a guy likes me or not," I said, grabbing the nearest cushion and hugging it to my chest. "That's why I wonder if I kinda brought this on myself."

Chantal punched me on the arm. "You're invoking the defense of every rapist on the planet. *'She asked for it.'* Or *'she dressed like a slut so she deserved it.'*" Chantal shook her head. "It doesn't work that way."

"I know, but..." Dave's accusations echoed in my head. Had I inadvertently led him on?

"But what?"

"He said a bunch of stuff—"

"That tried to lay the blame on you, right?" Chantal snorted. "Forget it, sweetie. None of this was your fault."

Chantal's cell beeped and she hesitated before picking it up.

"Go ahead." It would give me more time to ponder what the hell I was going to do.

I didn't want to throw my virginity away on some lowlife, but I wasn't holding out for the fabled knight in shining armor either. One thing I did know. Until I had sex for the first time, Dave's 'frigid bitch' and 'cockteaser' would haunt me.

"That was Reid," Chantal said, waving the cell at me. "He's coming over."

I sat bolt upright. "You didn't tell him anything?"

Chantal rolled her eyes. "Relax, I'm not a complete moron. I know your bro's overprotective. He'd probably bash that bastard's brains out and lose his fast track to the senate."

So true, and the major reason I'd already decided not to tell Reid about this. I loved my sole sibling dearly but since our dad ran out on us when he was seven Reid took his man of the house responsibilities very seriously.

"Then what's he doing in Vegas?"

"To see you, apparently." Chantal shrugged. "He said he'd been to your dorm, you weren't there, so he checked in here to see if I'd seen you."

"Why didn't he ring me?"

"Said he did."

I patted down the small purse I'd taken to the party, belatedly realizing I'd left my cell in my dorm room. "Damn."

Chantal poked me in the arm. "Rule number one of savvy women. Keep your cell within reach at all times."

She was right. I was a moron for leaving my cell behind when attending a party at a new place. Pity my street smarts weren't on par with my grades.

"I'm an idiot."

"Gullible idiot," Chantal added, with a smirk. "You need to find yourself a guy, sweetie. Pronto."

"Sure thing." I wriggled on the sofa and pretended to look under it. "Let me just pull one out of my ass."

Chantal laughed. "Maybe you should make that your summer project. Find a hot guy and let loose."

I wouldn't know where to start.

"What are you doing for summer?"

I grimaced. "No idea."

Chantal's hand flew to her mouth. "Tell me you're not spending it back home running around from wedding to wedding as your mom's lackey?"

"Are you nuts? I'm a sad case but I'm not that desperate."

Besides, been there, done that, ripped up the veil to prove it. Being an assistant to the most hyper wedding planner on the planet was not my idea of fun. I'd been roped into helping Mom too many times as a teenager. If I saw one more place card, garter or buttonhole rose, I'd scream.

"Then what are you going to do?"

A knock on the door saved me from answering. My brother always had impeccable timing. He was also incredibly astute so I better pull off the best acting of my life to fool him into believing there was nothing wrong.

"I'm not letting you off the hook," Chantal said, before she headed to the door.

The moment I heard my brother's booming voice, I wanted to cry. Stupid, but he was the one guy in this world I could count on.

"Hey, Sis." He strode into Chantal's lounge room, immediately shrinking it with his presence.

Reid had that effect everywhere he went. It wasn't the slick suits he wore or his height or his confidence he wore like a badge of honor. Simply, Reid was a guy people noticed because he had that unidentifiable 'it' factor. Pity I'd only inherited the 'shit' factor.

"Hey you." I stood and welcomed his hug, swallowing the lump in my throat. "What are you doing here?"

"Trying to find you." He eased away, held me at arms' length. "Got any plans for the next month?"

Was this a trick question? Did my powerful politician brother going places know what a loser he had for a sister?

"Why?" My eyes narrowed. "Because no way am I spending my summer in some cramped campaign office in LA folding letters or stuffing envelopes."

"Do you have plans or not?" His smug grin signaled he definitely knew something I didn't.

"No," I said, with a huff. "Not yet."

"Good." He pulled a folded document out of his inside top pocket and handed it to me. "Take a look at that and see if you'd like to join me."

"Hurry up, slow coach." Chantal elbowed me and I jostled her back as I unfolded the paper. "What is it?"

I sped read the document, not quite absorbing the impact. "This is an itinerary for a trip to Australia?"

"Yeah. One day in Melbourne. Two in Sydney. Then four weeks in far north Queensland." Reid folded his arms and smiled at me like a benevolent god. "You in?"

My mouth must've gaped because Chantal placed her finger under my chin and shut it.

"How? Why?" My brother had never played pranks on me when we were kids and by his benevolent expression, he was serious.

"My boss's daughter is the widow who runs the cattle station we'll be staying at in Queensland. He wants me to present a few proposals to facilitate ties between the cattle industries in Australia and California. He wants to get the farmers in Cali onside and some good PR happening for us. It'll be a huge boost to our next campaign."

This still sounded too good to be true. "Why can't he do it?"

"Because he wasn't so supportive when his only kid left the States to live in the outback twenty-five years ago and they've only reunited two years back when her husband died." Reid shrugged. "He doesn't want to mix business with family stuff, especially when they were estranged for so long."

"So you're his lackey?"

Reid nodded. "Yeah. A very lucky lackey who gets to visit Australia for the first time, all expenses paid, and take his sister because he's too busy to have a girlfriend."

"And because he's a lame-ass," Chantal piped up, flashing a sickly sweet smile at Reid when he flipped her the bird.

I scanned the itinerary again, not quite believing this was true. "You're serious?"

Reid nodded. "As deadly as those tiger snakes and funnel web spiders they have Down Under."

I didn't give a flying fig about the local fauna. A free trip to OZ? I'd grab my ruby slippers. I was so there.

"I'm in." I hugged Reid, who squeezed me back. He gave the best bear hugs. "Thanks."

"Want me to give you a ride back to the dorm so you can pack?"

I shot a panicked glance at Chantal. No way did I want to risk running into Dave and the resultant fallout if Reid was with me.

"When are you leaving?" Chantal slung an arm around

my shoulder. "Because we'd planned on having a girls' night in, so maybe she can pack tomorrow."

Reid glanced at his watch. "I've got the company jet ready to take us back to LA now, Sis, and we fly out tomorrow." He gave Chantal a noogie. "So your girls' night will have to wait."

Chantal mouthed 'I tried' behind Reid's back and I flashed a grateful smile. Hopefully, Dave would be hiding out in his room and we wouldn't cross paths.

"Okay then, let's go." I hugged Chantal, who whispered in my ear, "Aussie guys are hot. Chris, Liam and Luke Hemsworth? Alex O'Loughlin? Simon Baker? Find a lookalike and lose the cherry, okay?"

I stifled a laugh, not sure whether to be mortified my cousin knew I was a virgin or a tad excited by the prospect of being surrounded by Hemsworth lookalikes.

As we left, Reid rested his arm across my shoulder. "Ready for an outback adventure, Jessie?"

"Absolutely."

A month in Australia, an ocean away from UNLV and Dickwad Dave?

Bring it on.

6

JACK

"Kid, not only are you easy on the eye, you're a genius in the kitchen." Mrs. Gee ruffled my hair as she licked lemon curd I'd whipped off the spoon.

Heat crept into my cheeks. "Should I be worried you're unsheathing hidden cougar claws?"

She threw an empty plastic canister at my head in response.

Ducking, I laughed. "So you think I'm ready?"

"Ready?" She gestured at the afternoon tea feast I'd done from scratch, with her supervising. "You'll have me out of a job if I'm not careful."

I didn't have the heart to tell her there'd never be a chance of that, since I wouldn't be sticking around. Putting down roots in one place wasn't my style, no matter how much I liked learning from her.

"Your scones are light and fluffy. Your apple tea cake is sublime. Your plum jam is the best I've ever tasted." She pointed at the last item, my pride and joy. "And that red velvet cake you made especially for the Yanks is indescribable."

"Thanks," I said, my simple gratitude not nearly enough for what Mrs. Gee had done for me.

She'd given me an opportunity, had seen something in me that I never knew I had. The ability to create.

I'd scoured her cookbooks. I'd experimented with recipes. And I'd adlibbed a hell of a lot. The result? I actually believed I could cook. Not just serve rote learned basic meals to the station workmen, but actually cook fancy-schmancy dishes anyone would enjoy. Who knew?

"You did good." She beamed at me, pride making her eyes gleam.

Why couldn't I have had a normal mum like her? Not some flake that couldn't handle motherhood so she dumped her kid in a foster system that made me grow up way too fast.

"When are they arriving?"

As if on cue, I heard the distant rumble of a diesel engine and the clattering as one of the homestead's 4WDs traversed the metal grate at the entry to the property.

"That'll be them." Mrs. Gee untied her apron, dusted off her hands and patted her wiry grey curls. "Doreen wants the main staff to greet them. And what the boss lady wants, we do."

I turned away to check on the table one last time when she tapped me on the shoulder. "That includes you now."

What the fuck? I didn't want to be part of some pansy-arsed greeting party for the guests. This wasn't the eighteenth century.

"I'll give it a miss—"

"No, you won't." Mrs Gee actually twisted my ear. Hard.

"Ow." I rubbed it, much to her amusement. "That's harassment."

She winked. "Lucky for you, it's not of the other kind."

"Gross," I muttered, and she laughed out loud.

"Whip that apron off before I do it for you," she said, her outrageous teasing making me feel like I finally belonged.

"Slave driver," I said, doing as she said, and following her out the back door onto the bullnose verandah that surrounded the entire homestead.

We headed to the front, where Doreen and Gladys, the housekeeper who kept the homestead clean and the bedrooms stocked, stood near the front door, shading their eyes with their hands to watch the car approach.

"Who picked them up?"

Mrs. Gee smirked. "Bluey."

"Hope the Yanks appreciate a good bull castration story," I said, wondering what the politician and his girlfriend thought of the station manager's bluntness. I'd heard more than my fair share of Bluey's gory tales including calves stuck during birthing, dissecting snakes to eat their insides and the self-amputation of his toe when it got impaled on barb wire. The American tourists wouldn't know what hit them.

"Considering Bluey's love of discussing cattle's gonads, they will now." Mrs. Gee straightened as the car stopped not far from us and Bluey hopped out to open the back door.

"Should we break into the Star Spangled Banner now or later?" I muttered.

"Ssh," she said, shooting me a disapproving glare. "Behave."

"Yes, Mum." That softened the tension pinching her mouth as her attention returned to the guests.

A girl stepped out of the car first and my first impression? Yowza.

She wouldn't last a day out here let alone a month.

Pale skin. Brunette. Big brown eyes that darted around like she expected to be attacked by a rampant freshwater croc at any second. And she wore sandals. Pink, open-toe, strappy things best suited to the city. The color matched her loose dress perfectly, but what was underneath that shapeless thing intrigued me more.

She had curves. Nice ones.

And that's when her boyfriend got out of the car, giving me a hard dose of reality.

Stop checking out the young American chick. She's off limits.

Doreen stepped forward and shook hands with the dufus. "Nice to meet you, Reid."

"Likewise." Reid's white-toothed smile was more blinding than the sun. "And I'd like you to meet my sister, Jess."

Sister?

"Don't even go there, kid," Mrs. Gee said under her breath, so softly I wondered if I'd imagined the warning.

"She's not my type," I said, managing to sound like I meant it.

As if she had some inbuilt radar homing in on lying pricks, the girl turned her head slightly and her curious gaze locked onto me.

Her eyes widened. Her lips parted. Her cheeks flushed a pink to match her dress.

And my cock twitched.

"Keep your snake in the cage, Jack." Mrs. Gee gave me a none too gentle shove forward when Doreen beckoned us.

Fuck, what was it about women of any age and their ability to read minds?

The closer I got to the brunette, the more my skin prickled like the time I'd eaten too many kiwi fruit and had an allergic reaction. Maybe I was allergic to cute brunette's who couldn't stop staring at me too?

The stupid thing was, the closer we got, the more I wanted to touch her. Tug on her ponytail. Ruffle her cool exterior.

She looked too...*pristine* to be out here. Like a delicate exotic orchid against the harsh outback.

Which was plain dumb, because for all I knew she could be a ball breaker.

I shook the politician's hand when Doreen introduced us, but not much registered beyond the fact the guy was young, probably only a few years older than me, yet the socio-economic gap between us was huge.

"And this is Jess," Doreen said, her curious gaze swinging between us. "Meet Jack McVeigh, our new chef extraordinaire."

Did the missus have heatstroke? Because I wasn't an extraordinary anything, least of all a chef. A half-arsed cook willing to learn and experiment? Maybe.

"Pleased to meet you, Jack." The moment Jess's hand touched mine I wanted to yank back. Her hand was cool despite the late afternoon heat, but she somehow managed to send a sizzle up my arm.

It should've jumpstarted my brain and flashed huge warning signals like 'stay the fuck away.' Instead, I deliberately held onto her hand a tad longer than polite, wanting to see if I could rattle her as much as she'd rattled me.

Her gaze locked on mine and what I saw blew my mind.

Interest. Tempered with a healthy dose of curiosity and fear.

Well, that made two of us, because the kind of instant attraction I'd just experienced with a girl out of my league and off limits? Frigging terrifying.

"Enjoy your stay," I muttered, managing to sound rude and condescending, as I frowned, released her hand and stepped back.

She raised an eyebrow, imperious and cool. And I'd never wanted to unsettle someone as I did her at that moment.

"Jack's prepared a fabulous afternoon tea," Doreen said, ushering them inside. "Let's eat."

"Let's," Jess said, shooting me an indecipherable glance from beneath her lashes, and in my warped, lust-filled haze, I almost thought she wished she could eat me.

Fuck, this was going to be a long four weeks.

7

JESS

Four, long weeks of seeing *him* every day?

My cheeks flushed at the thought as I tried to chew and swallow a piece of cake. Red velvet. My favorite. Not that he could've known. But it seemed like some great, screwed up, cosmic sign.

That the first time I'd ever felt like jumping a guy, he was an outback cook with a bad attitude.

This was all Chantal's fault, putting stupid ideas about hot Aussie movie stars into my head. Because the fact was, Jack did look like Chris Hemsworth. A lot.

Dark blond hair. Startling green-blue eyes. Requisite stubble. Tall. Tanned. Broad-shouldered. Bad boy to the bone.

Damn. Bad analogy. I couldn't think about bone and Jack in the same sentence without squirming.

When he'd spoken in that deep, gravelly voice and

touched my hand? I'd felt like...like...stripping off and climbing all over him.

Had to be jetlag. A whirlwind day in Melbourne and two in Sydney hadn't been long enough to readjust my body clock.

Yeah, must be jetlag. I needed a week, maybe two, to get with the program. A program that didn't involve crushing on hot Aussie bad boys with equally bad attitudes.

Reid and Doreen's conversation washed over me as I sat at the dining table, wondering if I could sneak into the kitchen to see if my reaction to Jack had been a one-off.

For someone who hadn't had a lot of experience with guys, I couldn't understand what was so special about him. Discounting his rugged good looks and sexy Aussie accent, why was I obsessing over a guy I'd just met? A guy I'd barely see over the next four weeks.

"I'll need to spend more time in Sydney next week for business and was hoping it's okay if Jess stays here?"

Reid's question filtered through and recaptured my attention. My brother hadn't mentioned dumping me in the outback while he schmoozed in the city. Then again, considering the phonies he hung out with, think I'd rather take my chances out here.

Doreen nodded, but a small frown creased her brow. "That's fine, but I won't be around either. I've got my quarterly meeting scheduled with the financial planner in Brisbane."

"Don't worry. In that case, Jess can travel with me and we'll come back after I finish business." Reid glanced across at me and I glared while shaking my head.

Doreen laughed. "Jess looks like she'll be happier here."

"Jess would," I said, earning more laughter.

"If it's okay with you, Reid, she could stay here?" Doreen

pointed toward the kitchen. "Mrs. Gee lives in, as does Gladys, our housekeeper—"

"That sounds great," I said, my overt enthusiasm earning an eye roll from Reid and a compassionate smile from Doreen. "No offense, Reid, but given a choice between Sydney or here? The outback wins hands down."

Reid hesitated and I continued, "Besides, how much trouble can I get into out here? Surely it'd be safer than having me traipse around Sydney, spending way too much of your money while I shop during the day and checking out the clubs at night—"

"You're not legal," he said, sounding triumphant.

Doreen cleared her throat and hid her smile behind her hand. "Actually, here in Australia, Jess is legal. Our teens can go clubbing and drink at eighteen."

I knew my brother. He'd been protecting me since Dad walked out on us so no way would he like the thought of me exploring a strange city on my own, let alone at night while he was busy with his long dinners.

"You sure you want to stay here on your own?" Reid's dubious expression meant he was still torn, so it was up to me to make his mind up for him.

"I won't be alone. There's Mrs. Gee and Gladys."

And Jack.

How much I was looking forward to seeing more of him? That was on a strict need to know basis.

"Plus after spending all semester indoors listening to lecturers, I'd love to get some fresh air." And now, for the sealer. "With my student loans, it's going to be a lifetime 'til I get back here, if ever, so I'd really like the chance to enjoy it."

I must've inserted the right amount of pleading into my

tone because Reid finally nodded. "Okay, Sis. You're on your own." He jabbed a finger at me. "But behave."

He grinned at his own joke, knowing that was one instruction he didn't have to issue. I always behaved. I never did anything wrong.

With a hot Aussie guy roughly my age that had 'trouble' invisibly tattooed on his broad chest? Definitely time I stepped out of my comfort zone to see how much fun I could have if I misbehaved.

8

JACK

Dusk was my favorite time of the day.

When I'd dished up the last meal to the workers, scrubbed the last pot and rinsed the last pan, I could finally relax. Head back to my self-contained shack about half a mile from the homestead, crank up the classic rock I liked and kick back.

But first, a shower to wash off the grime of the day. It was my ritual, something I savored, because I'd never been able to relax during a shower at any of the foster homes I'd grown up in.

Being naked in a stranger's house always made me feel vulnerable. And that's what every house I'd been shunted to felt like: a stranger's place. I'd never felt at home in any of them, not even the three years I'd spent in outer western Sydney with a family who appeared surprisingly normal on face value. But the Ainsworths had their hang ups like the rest and I never felt anything other than what I was. The outsider. The interloper. Being welcomed at the dinner table for the simple fact having me there meant the family received a payout from the government.

It sucked. And while I hadn't endured some of the degrading stuff other foster kids put up with in exchange for a roof over their heads, I always felt vulnerable. Like my entire life could come crashing down on my head at any time.

Like I did every night, I glanced around. Yeah, like anyone would be taking a stroll around the station at this time of evening, just waiting until I made use of the outdoor shower. But old habits died hard and once I confirmed I wouldn't be accosted by a stray wallaby or rabid wombat, I cranked the shower lever, tested the water and stripped.

I liked that the shower stall only came up to my waist. Enhanced the feeling of openness, of being one with nature. Corny shit, I know, but every evening I did this felt frigging great.

I stepped under the tepid stream and tipped my head back. The moment I particularly enjoyed as part of my ritual because I got to see the billion stars starting to twinkle in the clear mauve sky.

There was no sky on earth like the outback sky. Not that I'd traveled much but the sky in Sydney wasn't a patch on this. And somehow, when I looked up at the stars every night, I reckoned I deserved this after all the years I'd showered in a hurry so I wouldn't be caught out.

I lathered up, taking my time as I always did despite the rationed water. Yeah, I definitely deserved this.

A noise captured my attention, the crunch of gravel underfoot, and I glanced over my shoulder. And froze.

Jess.

Taking a dusk stroll, rounding the corner of my shack.

This was my place. My down time. Last thing I needed was little Miss Prim and Proper muscling in. Her type may think they owned the place but she should be in the homestead where she belonged, sipping chamomile tea and watching soppy chick flicks.

"What the hell are you doing here?" I turned off the water, belatedly realizing my predicament.

My towel hung on the outside railing. In front of my shack. A good twelve feet away.

"I like walking at this time of evening." She shrugged, unable to tear her gaze away from my chest. "After spending all day in lecture theatres, it's great to clear my head."

Figured. She was probably a brainiac too. "You're at university?"

"Yeah, University of Nevada, Las Vegas. I'm a freshman." She wrinkled her pert nose as if she'd smelled something nasty. "But I'd much rather be here right now."

"Let me guess. Boyfriend troubles?"

I didn't want to engage in conversation with her, but I had to admit she piqued my curiosity, because she hadn't been afraid to take a stroll in the semi darkness in the outback on her first night here.

"I'd need to have a boyfriend for there to be trouble," she muttered, a frown appearing between her brow. "What's it like?"

"Having a boyfriend? Couldn't tell you. I'm straight."

Her frown eased and a smile tugged at the corners of her mouth. A mouth I suddenly couldn't look away from. "I meant showering outdoors."

"Care to try?" I laid my hand on the stall knob and she took a step back.

I laughed. "Not that adventurous, huh?"

She squared her shoulders and her head tilted up. "Maybe I am?"

So she didn't like being taunted? I'd have to remember that. Because a guy could have a shitload of fun teasing someone like her.

"I doubt it." I turned the knob and her eyes widened. "I guess we're about to find out how adventurous you really are."

"What are you doing?"

I grinned. "Getting my towel."

Her frantic gaze darted around at the same time I opened the stall door.

"It's behind you, in case you were wondering," I drawled, trying not to laugh at her obvious discomfort.

I shouldn't tease her, I really shouldn't. She was a guest. Off limits. But that urge to ruffle her poise when we'd first met this afternoon was back, stronger than ever.

And just when I thought she would turn tail and run, she surprised me.

"Go ahead and get it." Her gaze drifted from my chest, lower. "Wouldn't want you getting cold or anything."

Fuck. She'd called my bluff. As for getting cold? The only thing I was getting behind this stall door was hot. Extremely hot. And hard.

"Last chance, sweet thing." I swung open the stall door so slowly the hinges squeaked. "Leave now or cop an eyeful."

She met my gaze, hers challenging and defiant. "Do I look like I'm going anywhere?"

In retaliation, I pushed the stall door open the rest of the way, so hard it slammed against the side of the shower.

I stood there. Hands on hips. Daring her to look her fill.

And she did. Staring at me in open-mouthed wonder.

I should've felt self-conscious. I didn't. I felt like a frigging king, on top of the world, having a girl like her look at me like I was the best thing she'd ever seen.

The longer she stared at my cock, the harder I grew, until I was pointing straight at her.

Only then did she turn away, but not before I saw her press her hands to her cheeks and mouth 'wow.'

"If you fancy another peep show, I'm here every day. Same time," I called out at her retreating back.

She paused, and glanced over her shoulder, her smile impish. "Seen it once, seen it all before."

With that, she sauntered away, leaving me with a hard-on that wouldn't quit, and the distinct urge to run after her so she could do something about it.

9

JESS

I didn't like cooking. I'd done enough of it when I lived at home because Mom was too self-absorbed to ensure her kids ate. That, and the fact Mom's cooking tasted like reheated trash.

I could do the basics like cheese omelets, jar pesto tossed through pasta and a grilled steak. And at college, I survived on cheap noodles and cafeteria food. So the meals dished up at the homestead in one day? Divine.

And the fact I wanted to know whether Jack was the whiz concocting the culinary delights made it pretty damn hard to stay out of the kitchen. But I had to. Because if I pushed through that door and saw him again, I'd combust on the spot.

He'd kept me up all night.

How dare he strut around naked so I couldn't get the image of him out of my head? The fact he'd given me fair warning but I'd stuck around regardless was beside the point. There was something about that cocky, insufferable Aussie that rubbed me up the wrong way.

He brought out something in me I'd never thought I possessed.

My inner smartass.

I never traded quips with guys. I didn't backchat or spar or play word games. Yet in twenty-four hours, Jack had made me do it—and how.

I'd seen his penis. A very impressive penis. Erect.

And I'd never forget the sight of my first as long as I lived.

That's the thing about being a virgin. I'd kissed guys, I'd fooled around a little, but I hadn't actually seen the equipment. Now that I had? It was all I could think about.

"Pass the coffee, Jess."

Were all guys that big? Or did it only look that huge because it had been hard?

"Jess? Coffee?" Reid's voice finally penetrated my intent mental study of male anatomy and I glanced up.

"What?"

"Cof-fee puh-lease," he annunciated with exaggerated slowness and I finally got the message.

"Here." I passed him the pot and shook my head when he offered me a top up.

"Still jetlagged?"

"No, just a bit tired." Mentally fixating on a guy's dick all night would do that to a girl. "Long semester."

"How's it all going?"

I rolled my eyes. "You ring me weekly to get updates so nothing's changed."

Apart from the fact my best study partner and friend at college had tried to get it on with me.

Reid stabbed a piece of blueberry pancake with his fork and waved it at me. "You should be nicer to me. I brought you here, didn't I?"

"That's only because you're a lame ass for not having a girlfriend."

He laughed. "Long days at the office aren't conducive to a relationship."

Despite my teasing, I admired Reid. For a young guy, he was going places. I had no doubt he'd make it to the House of Representatives one day, which was his dream.

"And before you ask for the hundredth time this morning, I'll be fine here next week when you head to Sydney."

More than fine, if I persisted in taking strolls around the property at dusk.

Reid poured more maple syrup on his pancakes. "Jack seems like a good kid."

Uh-oh. I didn't like where this conversation was headed, especially as the mere mention of Jack made my cheeks flush.

"We only met him yesterday. How do you know?"

He shrugged. "Meet a lot of people in my profession from all walks of life. I can tell the good guys from the bad."

Wonder if my brother would re-evaluate his opinion if he knew Jack had showed me his penis a few hours after we met?

"Reckon he'd be good summer crush material." Reid winked and I choked on my OJ.

He laughed as I coughed and spluttered. "Just don't go falling too hard, Jessie girl. Guys like that are heartbreakers."

I dabbed at my mouth with a napkin and glared. "Make up your mind. One minute he's a good guy, the next he'll break my heart."

Reid held up his hands. "Just saying it'll be good for you

to have a little fun while you're here after a long semester." He paused, and mock frowned. "But not too much fun."

"Yes, Sir." I saluted and he grinned at my sass.

"Speaking of Jack, Doreen said he'd be happy to show us around. Take us on a few tours around the place, that kind of thing."

And just like that, the OJ I'd managed to swallow curdled in my stomach. I didn't want to hang out with Jack. Not after what I'd seen. And wanted to see again.

"Great," I managed to say when the silence grew. "This is an amazing country. Can't wait to explore."

I sounded weird, like I had a frog in my throat, and Reid studied me. "You okay?"

"Just peachy," I said, wishing my big-hearted brother hadn't put the notion of a summer crush into my head, wishing Jack didn't look like Chris Hemsworth, and wishing I hadn't seen him naked.

Okay, so that last wish? So not true.

"I'm done." Reid patted his stomach and pushed back from the table. "I need to call the Cattle Council of Australia to start negotiations, so I'll see you later."

"Knock yourself out." I waved him away, secretly admiring how driven he was and wishing I had half his ambition.

But after he left the dining room, I felt weird sitting there by myself. I'd learned that formal, sit-down meals were the norm at the homestead but I wasn't some lady of the house who had to be served.

I stood and cleared the dishes, stacking them on my arm before I headed for the kitchen. I pushed through the hinged door and my precarious plate-balancing act almost came undone as I spied Jack, bolting out the back door as fast as his long, lean legs could carry him.

Resisting the urge to stick my tongue out at his back, I entered the kitchen. When Mrs. Gee straightened from having her head stuck in a giant fridge, her eyes bulged out of her head.

"What do you think you're doing, Missie?" She bustled toward me like an angry hen, all puffed up and outraged. "Give me those dishes this instant and you head back in there and relax."

I laughed. "I live in a dorm on campus where I come from, so cleaning up is second nature."

She faltered. "But you're a guest...it's not right."

I placed the dishes in the sink. "Considering I'll be the only person in this house next week, apart from you and the other workers, how about we drop the formalities now and become friends?"

I watched the older woman deflate before my eyes.

She plucked at the frayed pocket on the front of her apron. "You'd rather hang out with me than surf the Net or lie around with an e-reader all day?"

"Sure." I pointed at the stove, where she had a delicious broth simmering. "You can give me some pointers."

Her eyebrows rose in unison. "You like to cook?"

"Not really, but a girl has to eat."

A knowing glint made her beady brown eyes glow. "Or is there another reason you want to hang around the kitchen?"

I shook my head, cursing my blushing cheeks. "I just think it'd be better if I ate in here with you while the others are away rather than sitting alone in that formal dining room."

"Makes sense." Mrs. Gee studied me for a few more seconds before turning away to busy herself with rinsing dishes. "Jack will be back in a minute. He's out picking herbs for the pumpkin soup he's making for lunch."

"So he does some of the cooking too?" I tried to instill the right amount of nonchalance in my tone but it still sounded desperate to me.

"All of it since you've arrived."

Impressive.

She paused, and glanced over her shoulder at me. "Why? Anything you fancy in particular?"

She was onto me. And there was nothing I could do but smile and shrug.

Mrs. Gee's wrinkled face creased further when she smiled too. "Word of warning. Jack's easy on the eye but he's not for you."

Sheesh. What was it with people around here? First Reid, now Mrs. Gee. Was I that easy to read? Could they see the invisible 'I SAW JACK NAKED AND WANT MORE' tattooed on my forehead?

Keeping my voice devoid of emotion, I said, "I'm here for a vacation, that's it."

"Smart girl." Mrs. Gee nodded and returned to her dishes.

The fact I had a sudden urge to check out the herb garden? Not so smart.

∼

"Is that dill or rosemary?" I had no interest in herbs but it seemed as good an opening line as any, considering the last time I'd seen this guy I'd seen his man bits.

"Neither. It's thyme." Jack slowly straightened from a squatting position and stared at me, a slow grin easing across his face. "Surprised to see you here."

"Why? I live here for the next month, remember?"

"Oh, I remember." His gaze started at my flip-flops and

traveled upward in a slow, leisurely perusal that made my skin prickle all over. "I just meant I'm surprised to see you out here when I thought I'd next see you at dusk this evening down by my shack."

I blushed, heat scorching my cheeks at the memory of what I'd seen last night.

He laughed. "So what're you going to dare me to do today?"

"Last night wasn't a dare," I said, sounding like a sulky kid. "You're just an exhibitionist."

His naughty grin alerted me to the fact he'd always win in any war of words we had. "When I had such a captive audience, do you blame me?"

"And you're a show off."

"You seemed to appreciate what I had to show off."

He had me there. The way I'd stared at him? Like I hadn't seen an erection before. Which I hadn't. But he didn't need to know that.

"Can we just forget about it?"

He raised an eyebrow. "I don't know. Can you?"

"Ego, much?"

Then again, with the size of what I'd seen, he had every right to be proud.

"Tell you what I'll do." He plucked a bunch of parsley and added it to the thyme in his other hand. "I won't mention it again if you stop looking at me like that."

"Like what?"

He crossed the small herb garden to stand close. Way too close, as he leaned in to murmur in my ear. "Like you want to do more than look."

His warm breath fanned my cheek and I sighed, my body alternating between tingling and flushing. I liked having him this close to me, liked the way he made me feel.

Jack made me feel like I could do anything and not be sorry.

Then he chuckled and broke the intimacy surrounding us. Of course he was teasing, trying to get me flustered. Screw him.

I stepped away and mustered my best haughty glare. "You wish."

"You have no idea what I wish for, sweet thing, and if you did–" he touched my arm, the barest brush of a fingertip, and I almost moaned, "–you wouldn't be standing there all prim and proper like butter wouldn't melt in your mouth."

I shouldn't encourage him, I really shouldn't. But this word play thing we had going on? Like nothing I'd ever done before with a guy. It was a serious turn on.

"What would I be doing?"

His fingertips trailed up my arm in a slow, deliberate caress that made me shiver with longing. "You'd be naked." He toyed with my bra strap, slipping a finger underneath to snap it. "In my bed." He skimmed my collarbone, precariously close to my breast, and I couldn't breathe. "Begging for more."

With that, he headed back into the kitchen, leaving me hot and shaking and yearning.

10

JACK

I'd managed to avoid Jess for five days.

And it looked like the feeling was entirely mutual.

She hadn't ventured near my shack again and whenever she was around the homestead I made sure I had urgent kitchen duties.

I couldn't be alone with her.

We'd spoken a grand total of three times: during introductions, at my shack when she'd seen me naked and in the herb garden. Each and every time I'd wanted to make the uptight princess lose control.

What was it about her air of untouchability that made me want to touch her real bad?

That wouldn't be such a great idea so I'd been a chickenshit and avoided her instead. The crazy part? Even though we'd only sparred twice, I actually missed it.

I liked that she had a wicked tongue beneath that cool

exterior. I'd love to discover exactly how wicked her tongue could be.

"Am I disturbing you?" Reid stepped onto the back verandah, looking every inch a smooth politician in his beige chinos, blue button down shirt and spotless brown boots. It was like the Yank had searched 'classic outback gear' on the Net and bought an outfit to suit the occasion.

He wasn't a bad bloke and we'd made small talk a few times, but being near a guy so put together made me feel like a failure.

"No, I'm taking a breather," I said, jerking a thumb at the small cooler near the kitchen door. "Help yourself to a drink."

"I'm fine, thanks." He sat next to me on the dusty top step and braced his elbows on his knees. "How long have you worked here?"

"About four months."

"It's an amazing country." Reid's gaze swept the panorama before us. The red dusty road, the paddocks, the mountains in the distance. "I envy you."

That'd be a first. Not many blokes of his caliber would envy a drifter cook with no ties to anyone or any place.

"From what I hear, LA would be a buzz compared to this place."

He nodded. "LA's great, but I grew up in a small town about an hour out of Vegas and I kind of miss the landscape." He pointed to the heat shimmering across the horizon. "See that? When I was a kid I used to think that magic happened at the end of the earth."

"And now?"

"Now I have to work my ass off to make anything happen let alone magic, I know it's a crock of shit."

I laughed, surprised by his candor. "Tell me about it. You don't get anywhere without working your arse off."

He grinned. "I love how you Aussies say arse for ass."

"And I love how you Yanks say cookie for biscuit, jelly for jam, and drop scone for pikelet."

"Touché." Reid cocked his thumb and forefinger and fired at me. "That's another thing I like. Your bluntness." He pointed at my slouching against a wooden post. "You're all so laid back."

Bet Reid wouldn't say that if he knew how frigging tense I was because of his sister.

"It's the heat," I said. "Hard to muster up the energy to do much of anything at the end of a long day."

Unless Jess came by my shack at dusk again...then I'd be raring to go.

"Know the feeling," Reid muttered, sounding less than impressed. "I put in long hours at the campaign office. Not much time for anything after that."

"So you don't have time to cruise Melrose and attend Hollywood premiers?"

He snorted. "You've been watching too much cable. I work. That's it."

"Doesn't sound like you enjoy it much?"

"I do but..." He swiped a hand over his face. "I've wanted to be in the senate for as long as I can remember. A governor toured my home town when I was about fourteen and I've wanted to make a difference ever since."

I sensed a major 'but' coming.

"I like the thought of having enough power to evoke changes but the long hours and lack of social life for a guy my age is a killer."

Ah, so that's what the Yank's problem was. He needed to get laid.

I knew the feeling.

"How old are you?"

"Twenty-three." Reid winced. "Listen to me, sounding like a sad ass. What about you?"

"What about me?"

Reid jerked a thumb over his shoulder at the kitchen. "You planning on cooking here for the rest of your life?"

"Nah. This is just a stop gap."

"Until?"

Until I figured out what the hell I wanted to do with my life. But a guy who had no qualifications and had spent the last four years moving around had limited options.

"Until I decide where I want to live and what I want to do." It was the closest thing to the truth and more than I could've imagined sharing with a guy I'd met a week ago.

But there was something about Reid Harper that encouraged me to let my guard down. He was one of the good guys. And despite our massive socio-economic differences, I could've imagined us being mates.

"What's to decide?" He pinned me with a speculative stare. "Jess tells me you've prepared all the meals since we've been here and they're fucking fantastic."

I didn't know whether to be happy or appalled Jess had been talking about me with her brother. But the very fact he was sitting here making idle chatter meant she hadn't told him everything about me.

"Thanks." I shrugged. "But it's something I do to earn a living, not a lifelong ambition."

Reid's eyes narrowed. "You've never done a formal apprenticeship?"

"Nope."

He made a little scoffing sound of disbelief. "Well, let me tell you. As someone who eats a lot of takeout because of my long work hours, and who spends the rest of the time at fancy dinners with contributors and campaign workers, your food on a scale of one to ten is a well deserving eight."

Embarrassment made me squirm. I wasn't used to praise let alone the admiration of someone like Reid. He had to be bullshitting me. But why?

"That's why I asked if you were trained, because…" Reid hesitated, as if unsure of my reception to his next words.

Considering I now thought he was full of shit, I didn't blame him. But I was curious.

"Because?"

"Feel free to tell me to butt the hell out of your life, but I'm heading to Sydney for work at the end of next week and one of my boss's campaign investors I have to meet with runs a restaurant there."

I had no idea where he was going with this. "That's great. It's a tough competitive market down there."

"He's Michelin starred, apparently. Great reputation." Reid hesitated again, before shooting me a speculative glance. "I could have a chat to him if you like. About an apprenticeship?"

Speechless, I stared at this guy I barely knew, willing to go out on a limb for me. My eyes must've bugged as big as saucers because he laughed.

"It's not that big a deal, but I really do think you've got talent and it'd be a shame for outback station workers to be the only beneficiaries of your food."

I wanted to thank him. Wanted to slug him on the jaw for putting ideas into my head I'd never contemplated and making me hope. Because what he'd just proposed? Could set me up for life.

If I got a trade behind me, became a real chef, I could go anywhere and be respected for my profession, rather than slumming it in dirty outback sheds dishing up the same old, same old to a bunch of unappreciative workers who ate for sustenance and energy rather than taste.

"I don't know what to say..." I stuck my hand out. "Thanks, mate."

Reid shook my hand. "Don't thank me yet, because it may not happen. But I reckon someone as good as you deserves a chance to shine."

We fell into a companionable silence as I absorbed the impact of possibly working under a Michelin-starred chef. I wouldn't get my hopes up but damn, it was hard not to.

"By the way, Doreen's going to Brisbane while I'm in Sydney, so that means Jess will be on her own here. Seeing as you're about the same age, do you mind keeping an eye on her?" Reid gestured at the landscape. "Maybe show her around, that kind of thing?"

Oh no. Hell no.

Because what sprang to mind when Reid said 'that kind of thing?' didn't involve playing tour guide. It involved me and Jess naked and writhing and sweaty.

Reid continued, oblivious to the fact I hadn't answered. "It'll be good for her to kick back for a while. See a bit of the countryside. She works too hard."

"Looks like that runs in the family."

Reid grinned. "Jess is the brainiac. I just use my big mouth to get by."

"So it's just the two of you?"

"Yeah. Our dad ditched us when I was seven. Mom raised us." His mouth softened into a smile. "Mom's loud and flamboyant and the bubbliest person you'd ever meet."

Which went a long way to explaining why her daughter was the opposite. If anyone knew our childhood shaped us,

I did. No prizes for guessing why Jess was quiet, aloof and reserved.

"You seem like a pretty cool family," I said, sounding way too wistful.

"What about your family?"

Thankfully, Mrs. Gee called out for me at that moment, saving me from having to hedge around the truth rather than give Reid my sorry arse tale.

"Duty calls." I stood.

"Sure." Reid stood too. "I'll definitely put in a good word for you in Sydney."

"Thanks." I shook Reid's hand again before I headed into the kitchen, pondering how funny life could be. After the B&S ball I'd been restless. Edgy. Lost.

Now I had a possible job opportunity and a woman driving me to distraction.

A woman I had to look after next week apparently, with her brother's blessing. A brother who was doing me a massive favor.

This could get complicated.

11

JESS

I'd taken enough photos to overload my cell in an effort to stop ogling Jack as he took us on an outback tour. But it was hopeless. I couldn't keep pretending like he didn't exist and if I didn't join in the conversation soon, Reid would think something was wrong. And it was. Majorly wrong. Because I couldn't stop thinking about the last time Jack had spoken to me, the way he'd touched me...

"How big is this place?" Reid shaded his eyes and peered through the windshield.

"About eighteen thousand hectares," Jack said, expertly steering the four-wheel-drive around potholes. "Equivalent to forty-five thousand acres."

"Shit. That's bigger than Craye Canyon."

I pretended to enjoy the geography lesson from the back seat. I preferred it back here. Much easier staring at the back of Jack's head than being next to him. Though the few times our gazes had locked in the rearview mirror? Bad enough.

I hadn't seen him much over the last week. He'd been avoiding me, which was just fine. I didn't want to see him, not after his parting comment the last time we'd seen each other.

He wanted me naked, in his bed, begging for more.

Combined with the visual I'd copped when he'd stepped out of that shower?

Sensory overload. Every time I closed my eyes, that's all I could see. We were in his bed, doing...things I wish I knew about.

I hated how inadequate he made me feel. Like he'd seen stuff and done stuff I could only dream about. It made me feel perpetually off-kilter and likely to do something crazy: as crazy as daring him to step out of that outdoor shower.

"The homestead's about one thousand feet above sea level, so that's why we get great views." Jack pointed to his right. "If you squint and take a look out there, you'll see the Great Barrier Reef."

I craned my neck, and could just glimpse a sliver of blue ocean.

"Careful you don't strain yourself rubbernecking," Jack said, his teasing drawl making me bristle.

Yep, even an offhand remark designed to make me laugh made me feel gauche instead.

Reid laughed. "Sis doesn't get to see ocean very often."

"Make that never, dufus," I said, wishing I could elbow my brother, hard. He wasn't helping me feel anything other than a small town girl way out of my depth.

"I'm guessing there isn't too much water in Nevada where you come from." This time, Jack's tone had softened, almost as if he sensed my discomfort and I flashed him a grateful grin when he glanced at me in the mirror.

"About the closest I've got in the last six months is a day trip to Hoover Dam with a couple of study buddies..." I trailed off, remembering Dave had been on that trip.

Dave, my friend. Who I'd trusted. Until he'd tried to put his penis inside me.

"What's wrong?"

Damn, trust Jack to pick up on that too. How did he do that when he hardly knew me?

"The bumpy roads are giving me bit of motion sickness."

Reid passed me a bottle. "Here, have some water."

"Do you want me to stop?" Jack's steady gaze bore into me. He didn't buy my lie for a second.

"No, I'll be fine."

As long as I blocked out Dave and didn't feel like hugging Jack one minute, slugging him the next.

"There's a cattle round-up happening ahead." Jack pulled the four-wheel-drive over and killed the engine. "Watch."

Grateful Jack had let me off the hook, I gawked as several highly trained kelpie dogs, along with station hands on horseback, rounded up a massive herd of cattle in what seemed like less time than it took me to get dressed in the morning.

"Wow, that was amazing," I said, practically bouncing up and down on the back seat in excitement.

"I'm just going to take a few long range photos," Reid said, opening the passenger door and stepping out.

Leaving me alone with Jack.

"Feeling better, I see." He rested his arm along the back of the seat and half turned to face me. "Just for the record?

You may have your brother fooled but I want to know the story behind those study buddies."

I clamped my lips tight and eyeballed him.

He chuckled. "I've got a great technique for loosening lips."

"I just bet you have," I snapped, hating when he smirked. "Too bad I'm not interested."

"Pity." He stared at my mouth. "I would've had a great time getting you to talk."

Thankfully, Reid got back into the car, ensuring smart-assed Jack had to shut his big mouth.

A mouth I wanted to kiss as badly as he wanted to kiss mine apparently.

And as we drove through the open savannah forest back to Cooweer Homestead, all I could think about was the two of us left to our own devices for the week ahead.

12

JACK

Mrs. Gee gave me the afternoon off for good behavior apparently. Not only had I wowed the guests with my culinary efforts, I'd earned some serious brownie points from my biggest critic.

She'd hovered over me the first few days when I'd been experimenting with her favorite recipes, giving advice when needed. I'd learned more about cooking in the last two weeks than I had in the previous twelve months when I'd cooked for sheep shearers, cane cutters and the occasional travelers' outpost.

If Reid Harper came through for me with that offer of an apprenticeship in Sydney, I'd be indebted to him and Mrs. Gee. If it weren't for her, I never would've had the opportunity to try cooking fancy stuff let alone have someone like Reid taste it, enjoy it and want to recommend it.

Reid had headed off this morning, along with Doreen.

Leaving the homestead to run as per usual. Stockmen taking care of the cattle, Bluey the station manager in charge of the everyday running, Gladys ensuring the household ran smoothly, Mrs. Gee and I doing the cooking.

And one pest of a houseguest who I couldn't stop thinking about.

If I had a rare afternoon off, I'd usually go for a horse ride. I liked the rush of galloping that would clear my head. And the solitude. But looked like I might have a hanger-on today.

"You going for a ride?" Jess propped in the doorway of the stable, looking way too tempting for someone who should be off limits.

Not that there was anything particularly sexy about her faded skinny jeans and red T-shirt, but it was the way she wore them. Comfortable in her own skin. Classy. And way out of my league.

"Yeah." I cinched the girth, checked the stirrups.

"Want some company?"

"Not really."

Rude? Hell yeah. But the last thing I needed right now was to be accompanied by the woman I wanted to get my hands on.

"Why? Afraid I'll show you up?" She sauntered into the stable, a determined glint in her eyes. Big, beautiful brown eyes that were fixed on me. "I didn't pick you for a coward."

Was she talking about the ride or something else? Like the fact every time we were within two feet of each other, we sparked, and I ran.

"What are you, twelve? Trying to use reverse psychology on me?" I patted the gelding's neck as the horse skittered slightly when Jess approached.

"God, you're full of yourself," she said, wrinkling her

pert nose like she'd just stepped in a pile of horse shit. "How about we forget the fact I saw your dick and get past it so we can hang out without any crap?"

She actually blushed when she said dick and I laughed. She was adorable. And I wanted her real bad.

"What if I don't want to get past it?" I threw it out there as a deliberate taunt, knowing she'd bolt if I harped on it. "What if I want you to remember it in vivid detail?"

I expected her to tell me to fuck off. I expected her to turn tail and run. I didn't expect her to take a step forward, invading my personal space, as she placed a hand on my chest.

"What if my memory's not that good and I need a reminder?" She stared up at me from beneath long lashes, her bravado making me want to kiss the smirk from her lips all the more.

"Already told you, swing by the shack at dusk any day."

"Maybe I will." She patted my chest in a strangely intimate gesture that made me want to haul her into my arms, back her into one of the empty stalls and demonstrate what a roll in the hay meant. "But for now, I'll settle for a ride."

I had two options. Blow her off—damn, bad analogy—or suck it up like a man. Another shitty analogy.

It wasn't her fault I wanted to get into her panties. Besides, Reid had asked me to look after her, show her some sights, that kind of thing. How would it look if Reid returned, asked Jess what she'd done and she said nothing because I'd been a bad-tempered prick?

"Fine," I said, sounding like a sulky brat. "I assume you can ride?"

"You'll see how well shortly, when I whip your ass in a race." She cocked her hip in challenge and damn if I didn't want to bend her over my knee and whip her arse for real.

"Confident, much?" I muttered, secretly pleased she could ride. Last thing I felt like doing was babysitting a newbie in the saddle.

"So which horse should I saddle up?" She wandered over to the stalls and that's when a new predicament struck.

The workmen were out on their mounts, one of the usual homestead rides was in foal, the other mare was due for shoeing and I had the gelding. Which left Doreen's stallion that no one touched on threat of castration.

"Sorry, I forgot, there's no spare mount at the moment," I said, feeling worse now than I had a few minutes ago when I'd refused her just to be churlish.

She tut-tutted. "You'll go to any lengths to avoid spending time with me."

"I'm not bullshitting you—"

"What about I ride pillion with you?"

Hell no. Having her taut little body pressed against me from behind, her arms wrapped around me, her crotch against my arse? A thousand times no.

"That wouldn't be fair on old Dundee." I patted the gelding's rump and he stood there, placid and expectant, contemplating the two idiotic humans with a slight turn of his head.

"He looks as strong as a draft horse," she said, stroking Dundee's neck with smooth, repetitive movement, making me wish she'd touch me like that.

My cock hardened. Not helping.

As if sensing the real reason behind my reluctance, she pinned me with a sassy stare. "Pity. Might be kinda nice for a shy, college girl like me to head home with tales of riding real close to a rugged, handsome Aussie."

I snorted and Dundee joined in. "Yeah, like flattery will make me change my mind."

Though her mention of college did spark my memory, something I'd wanted to ask her about since that tour I'd taken her and Reid on.

"Did some guy in college do a number on you?"

Her smile faded and I could've sworn she paled. "I don't know what you mean by doing a number?"

"Come on, Jess, don't pull the Aussie-ism versus Americanism card now. You know what I mean."

She tilted her head up in defiance and it made me want her all the more. "How do you know anything happened?"

"Don't do that." I jabbed a finger at her. "Don't treat me like I'm some hick, ignorant dickhead who can't read people."

When her lips compressed in a mutinous line, I stepped forward, close enough I could smell a soft floral fragrance. Lilacs. Delicate and elegant, like her.

If I'd hoped to intimidate her into telling me the truth, it didn't work, because she merely tilted her head back to glare at me.

Looked like I'd have to give a little to get a little back.

"Want to know how I got so good at reading people? Spend ten years in the foster system and you soon learn when arse-holes are lying to you or not."

Her expression softened. "What happened to your folks?"

"Dad shot through when I was four, Mum when I was six. I was a rotten brat." At least, that was the guilt trip Mum used to lay on me for the reason Dad left. What was her excuse?

Sadness downturned Jess's mouth. "I'm sorry."

She touched my arm and I tried not to flinch. I couldn't have her touching me, not when I wanted to touch her so badly I ached.

"I don't need your pity, but maybe now you can understand why I want to know what happened at your college?" Unable to resist, I snagged a strand of her hair and wound it around my finger. "And I know it's something bad by the way you completely shut down in the car when study buddies were mentioned."

"You're very observant," she said, her gaze transfixed on my finger as I wound her hair tighter and tighter before releasing it when I got too close to the tender skin above her ear.

"Occupational hazard." I scrunched up my face, pretending to think. "Having to keep the broccoli from bullying the beans, the squash from *beet*ing the pumpkin, get it?"

Her soft laughter made me want to hold her. "That's a woeful pun."

I touched her forearm and I swore I heard her sigh. "Tell me."

Indecisive, she nibbled on her bottom lip, and it took every ounce of my willpower not to do the same.

"Jess?" I slid my fingers down her forearm to her hand, where I threaded my fingers through hers.

I had no idea why I did it. I didn't go for handholding. Not that I had girlfriends long enough to do it.

"A guy I trusted, my closest study buddy, tried to rape me." Her flat, emotionless monotone spoke volumes. She'd tried to block it out.

I squeezed her hand so hard she yelped and I released her as rage consumed me. I wanted to beat the bastard to a pulp. Crush him without mercy. Kick his head in.

"It didn't get too far before I escaped, but the fact it happened in the first place?" She shook her head. "I'm such an idiot."

"No you're not—"

"I trusted that slime ball!" she yelled and Dundee sidestepped.

"Sorry, fella." She patted Dundee's neck. "I thought I knew him and I didn't know him at all, which really makes me doubt my own judgment."

Not only had this prick assaulted her, he'd made her question herself. I could definitely kill him with my bare hands.

"Nothing wrong with your judgment." I forced myself to relax, to allow my anger to dissipate. "You're here with me, aren't you?"

She managed a small smile, just as I intended. "So now you know. Happy?"

"Considering what I want to do to that fucktard for hurting you, I'm so far from happy it's not funny." I recaptured her hand. "But some good did come out of it."

"What?"

"We've moved past the outdoor shower scene moment and have actually connected as friends."

The moment the words tumbled from my mouth I wanted to slap myself upside the head. We weren't friends. We could never be anything more than passing acquaintances.

But having her trust me with something so important made me feel closer to Jess than I had to anyone in a long time, if ever.

"Friends." She shook my hand like a buddy, her tremulous smile making my heart do a weird jive. "Who ride pillion."

I laughed. "Lady, you drive a hard bargain."

"Cookie, you have no idea."

"Cookie?"

"My nickname for you. You cook, right?"

I'd never had a nickname before and it touched me. "Plus I'm sweet and delectable."

She rolled her eyes.

"And edible," I added, determined to get back onto familiar territory, with the two of us sparring with an underlying hint of sexuality.

Nicknames implied intimacy and closeness, two things I couldn't afford to have with Jess. No matter how much I might secretly crave them.

She released my hand and shoved me away. "Yeah, but like the real thing, too much will make me puke."

God, I loved how quick she was. I could easily fall for Jess as more than a friend, which would be the ultimate act in masochism.

She was leaving in two weeks. She was a girl so far out of my league I'd need a stepladder to get up there. And her brother was doing me a massive favor.

Three sane reasons to keep my distance.

Pity I'd never been any good at sanity.

13

JESS

When would I learn?

Daring Jack to let me ride pillion had been a deliberate ploy to rattle him at the time. But now? With my arms wrapped around him, my body on fire from our proximity and the pure male scent of him filling my senses? I was the one seriously rattled.

Not that the last ten minutes hadn't been exhilarating, galloping through the station's grounds and beyond, mile after mile of arid beauty. I didn't know where to look first so kept my cheek firmly pressed against Jack's back.

Now that we'd slowed to a trot, I could hear my thoughts again above Dundee's pounding hooves. And they weren't pretty.

Why did I blab all that stuff about Dave? I barely knew Jack and all we did was try to score points off each other. Yet when he'd said we were friends? I could've hugged him.

Having him share some of his past with me had precipitated my verbal diarrhea, I knew that, but how did it happen that I felt closer to Jack than I did with any of my college friends?

Two semesters at UNLV and I still couldn't name one person I would've told about Dave...bar Dave. And that's what irked the most, that the one guy I'd chosen to trust as a friend in my freshman college year had turned out to be anything but.

"We'll stop here and eat." Jack reined in Dundee near the bottom of a small valley and I let the peacefulness wash over me.

It was like Jack and I were the only two people in the world.

"You can let go of me now," he said, clearing his throat.

"And spoil my fun?" I gave him a tight squeeze, akin to a Heimlich maneuver, and chuckled when I heard his ooph.

I swung my leg over Dundee's rump and slid to the ground. My butt ached, my back twinged and my legs wobbled, but as I watched Jack's mighty fine ass as he dismounted, it was so worth it.

He turned and caught me staring, a slow grin spreading across his face. "What is it with you and my nether regions?"

Damn, I was busted. "Maybe they're so impressive I can't help but stare?"

"I'm flattered, but don't waste your time." He busied himself making Dundee comfortable, leaving me to ponder what he meant.

"A girl can't look?"

"Looking is fine. Touching isn't," he muttered, sounding increasingly grouchy as he gave Dundee a final pat and started setting out the picnic he'd packed.

"Why's that?"

He glanced up from the blanket he'd spread on the

ground. "Because I won't be your holiday fling."

Guess that meant I couldn't tell him he'd be my first, too. "Surprising."

His eyes narrowed. "Why? Because you think a bum like me would have sex with any woman who crossed my path?"

Wow, there was way more going on here than me making a flippant remark and him taking it out of context.

I held up my hands. "Whoa. PMS, much?"

Some of his tension eased as I glimpsed a flicker of a smile. "Sorry, you hit a nerve."

I wanted to know more, despite doubting the wisdom of prodding him when he was in a mood. "Because you've been sleeping your way across the east coast of Australia?"

"Something like that," he said, through gritted teeth, as he resumed laying the picnic out.

If I'd been curious before, I was positively intrigued now. Considering the Chris Hemsworth thing he had going on, I wasn't surprised he'd never lack for willing partners in bed. Jack was seriously gorgeous. But rather than being proud of the fact like most egotistical guys would be, he sounded...disgusted.

"And this is a problem because?"

"Drop it," he said, sitting on the edge of the rug and hugging his knees to his chest. "You don't see me asking you the number of guys you've been with."

"That's because there've been none," I muttered, stomping toward the rug and hating that I was insanely jealous of the number of faceless women he'd probably had amazing, rampant, climb-the-walls sex with.

He sat bolt upright, like the Eastern brown snakes I feared, courtesy of Bluey's descriptive lectures on our arrival, had bitten his ass. "What did you just say?"

"Nothing." Me and my big mouth. As if an experienced

guy like him would ever come near me now.

"You're a *virgin*?" He made it sound like I was an alien.

"So what?" I thrust my chin up, trying to stare him down. "Not everyone can be a man whore like you."

He winced and I was instantly contrite. "Sorry, that was out of line."

"The truth hurts," he said, picking up a loaf of bread and ripping great chunks off with his hands. "Not that I'm quite as bad as you make me sound, but I'm done with transient flings."

"Too bad," I said, deliberately droll, trying to get the conversation onto familiar teasing territory. "Would've been great to have an experienced guy like you take care of that little virginity problem I've got."

His gaze locked on mine and I could've sworn I saw electricity arc between us.

"You're not serious?" He stared at my mouth and I swallowed against the inane urge to leap over the picnic rug and kiss him.

"Deadly."

After what seemed like an eternity but in reality couldn't have been more than a few seconds, he swiped a hand over his face. Yeah, like that would wipe away the blatant yearning I'd just glimpsed.

"I'm not the guy for you, Jess," he said, holding his palms out to me like he had nothing to hide. "I'm not worth it."

"Do you actually believe that bullshit you're spouting or is it just an excuse because you're not really attracted to me?"

There, I'd voiced my number one insecurity when it came to guys, particularly this one. Was I attractive? I didn't have big boobs or long legs or hourglass curves. I had brown hair, brown eyes and was average height. When I looked in the mirror, I thought I looked okay. Nice. Which was about as bland as anyone could get.

"You're frigging nuts." He leaped to his feet and started pacing, scuffing at eucalypt bark with his worn boots. "What you saw after I showered? A damn good indication how attractive I find you."

Secretly thrilled, I shrugged. "Could've just been a physiological reaction. Don't you wake up with it like that?"

He muttered, "fuck," and continued pacing. "For someone who hasn't been with a guy, you sure know a lot about our working parts."

It was my turn to smile. Did he think I was that innocent he couldn't call a cock a cock?

"So you do think I'm attractive?"

In response he stopped a good eight feet away, as if scared I'd suddenly launch myself at him. "I'm not discussing this with you."

"Why?"

He pointed down below. "Because if we don't stop talking about it, I won't be able to get back on Dundee to make the return trip."

I stared at the obvious bulge in his jeans. "Oh."

"And in case you were wondering? I think that more than answers your question," he said, sitting on the rug as far from me as he could. "I can't even talk about being attracted to you without getting a hard-on."

"Considering you won't let me do anything about it, I guess we shouldn't talk about it then." I clasped my hands in my lap, the epitome of prim, when inside I was doing a happy dance.

A sexy, worldly guy like Jack was attracted to me.

Now I had to figure out how to change his mind about not coming near me.

14

JACK

I'm an idiot. A moron. A complete dickhead.

That's the only explanation for continuing to hang out with Jess.

As if the horse ride two days ago hadn't been torture enough. Physically, mentally and emotionally. It's damn uncomfortable riding with a hard-on, as I'd discovered the moment she swung up behind me, wrapped arms around me, and hung on like her life depended on it.

I'd felt every little shift in position she made, heard every little sigh. And savored the illicit contact like a parched guy stumbling across a billabong in a desert.

For despite taking a blatant stand about us only ever being friends, I wanted that sweet, sexy girl with every cell in my horny body.

As if there weren't enough reasons to keep my hands off, discovering she was a virgin topped my list of not getting involved. I was a bastard, but not so much of a bastard that I'd take advantage of her holiday crush.

I should've known. She wore that untouched air like her fine clothes. A hint of vulnerability beneath her sass. It was addictive.

And wrong.

Something I'd have to remember tonight, when I put myself through another torture session. Jess had invited herself over and I hadn't had the heart—or the balls—to say no.

We should've been uncomfortable after our revelations on the ride. Instead, we'd spent the last two days hanging out when I wasn't working. We'd talked about anything and everything from politics to religion to our favorite music. Which is what led her here tonight.

Jess was clueless about classic Aussie rock. I was going to indoctrinate her. My excuse; I was sticking to it.

A knock sounded at the door. "You in there, Cookie?"

That was another thing I liked but pretended not to. Having her call me Cookie seemed to solidify our bond.

"Door's open," I called out, waiting until she stepped into the shack before hitting play on my iPod.

I smirked as she jumped five feet when INXS's Original Sin ripped from the speakers.

"That's loud," she mouthed, covering her ears with her hands.

"Only way to listen to amazing music like this," I shouted, beckoning her in and kicking shut the door behind her. "You'll see."

"What?" She cupped her ear. "I can't hear you."

I grinned and cranked up the music, grabbed her hand and spun her around.

She laughed, a joyous sound that made my chest ache

with wanting her, so I settled for working out my frustration by dancing like a crazy person.

I lost count of the number of songs we danced to, and I couldn't help but admire a girl who matched me throughout Cold Chisel's Khe Sanh, Daddy Cool's Eagle Rock, and AC/DC's You Shook Me All Night Long move for move. She jumped and shimmied and bumped with me through Skyhooks, Australian Crawl, Mondo Rock, Hunters and Collectors, and Midnight Oil. She didn't know any of the songs but she didn't care. She got into the spirit of music idols triple our age, until we could barely breathe.

Then Crowded House's Don't Dream It's Over filtered through the speakers and I wanted to hit stop ASAP.

Slow dancing with Jess would kill me.

She must've seen the indecision on my face because she positioned herself between the iPod and me, ensuring I'd have to reach around her to shut the bloody thing off.

Then she went one step further.

She closed the distance between us, wrapped her arms around my neck and rested her cheek against my chest.

I couldn't push her away.

I had no choice but to wrap my arms around her waist, rest my chin on her head and just *feel*. Feel her heart pounding in rhythm with mine. Feel her soft curves. Feel her hair tickling my nose. Feel like I could do this forever.

We swayed together and I wanted to imprint this moment on my memory. Did I feel like a needy chick? Hell yeah. But this girl was special and I may not get another chance to hold her in my arms like this. In fact, I wouldn't. I couldn't.

When the last haunting strains of Neil Finn's voice faded, I eased back.

Our faces were so close. And damn if Jess wasn't staring

at me with blatant adoration, her cheeks flushed, her lips parted.

I wanted to kiss her. I should kiss her.

But I'd sworn I wouldn't give into mindless urges anymore, especially not with a girl who deserved so much more than I could give her.

"Thirsty?" I released her and turned away so I wouldn't have to deal with the hurt in her eyes. "We worked up quite a sweat."

She laid a hand on my shoulder. "Jack?"

I knew what she was asking. With that simple touch, she was asking what the hell was going on between us, but fucked if I could give her the answer she wanted.

"I'll get us a couple of soft drinks, unless you prefer beer?" I stepped away and she followed me.

"Soda's fine," she said, sounding surprisingly calm when I half expected her to push the issue with the way we'd danced. "Now that you've educated me with your music, time for me to educate you with iconic romantic movies."

"Chick flicks," I said, sounding suitably disgusted, when in fact I'd watched a few and enjoyed them. Wasn't much to do in the outback after dark so I went through DVDs like Mrs. Gee went through sugar. And I wasn't ashamed to admit I sniffled during The Notebook, my closet favorite.

"Not *a* chick flick. *The* chick flick," she said, as I returned to the pokey makeshift lounge room/bedroom to find her brandishing a DVD of Dirty Dancing. "Seen it?"

"What do you reckon?" I handed her a soft drink and grabbed the DVD while wrinkling my nose. "As you saw from my demonstration over the last half hour, I'm more of a slam dancing kinda guy."

"Pity. Something tells me you'd be real good at dirty dancing." Her gaze deliberately swept me from head to foot in a bold move that would've normally had me saying screw the movie and let me screw you.

Instead, I popped the DVD out of the cover and slid it into the player.

"No popcorn or chocolate?"

I glared at her. "I cooked you penne alla matriciana for dinner and you're still hungry?"

"That pasta was superb." She rubbed her stomach and I glanced away, instantly struck by how much I'd like to do the same. "But haven't you heard? Women have a second stomach for sweets."

"But you had a piece of pav too." I loved her appetite. Nothing sexier than a woman who appreciated her food. And continually told the chef how great it was.

"Fine, just turn on the damn movie." She folded her arms and pretended to sulk, which was exceptionally cute.

As long as the movie was all I turned on tonight.

Once I hit play, I sat. As far away from her as I could on the old plaid couch. I'd never cared how small the one room shack was before, but with Jess in it? Felt like the four walls constricted by the minute.

"God, I love this movie." Jess sighed, and curled her legs up beneath her as she sipped from her soft drink can.

Her gaze was riveted to the small flat screen TV for the duration of the movie, while I kept sneaking glances at her. And all the while, that lilac fragrance she wore wafted over me. It probably clung to my skin; we'd been dancing that close. Just one more thing to torture me.

By the time the credits rolled, I knew exactly why she loved this flick.

Innocent teen falls for older off-limits bad boy. Yet they had a happy ending. Go figure.

"So, what did you think?" She half turned away from me,

dabbing at the corners of her eyes with her pinkies, before turning back.

"Not bad."

"Not bad?" She screeched, swinging her arm wide to whack me in the chest. "That's like me saying to you that your Aussie rock is reasonably okay."

I clutched my chest and fell to the side like she'd wounded me. "You're comparing AC/DC to Patrick Swayze?"

"Neanderthal," she muttered, tilting her nose in the air in a pretend huff.

"You're cute when you're ruffled," I said, gazing up at her from my semi-upside down position on the couch.

"And you're obnoxious," she said, an insult defied by her sliding a fraction closer so I had no option but to rest my head in her lap.

Bad move. Catastrophic move. Being so close to nirvana and not being able to go there.

"But I kind of like you anyway." She ran her fingers through my hair, grazing my scalp, and a shiver shot through me. Who knew having her fingers in my hair could be so frigging erotic?

"Pity you can't emulate Patrick." She continued her rhythmic stroking and it felt so damn good I would've told her anything to have her continue.

"That's fictional, sweet thing, and sorry to say, this bad boy isn't about to turn good."

She stopped, her hand resting on my forehead, like she was testing if I had a fever. "What if this good girl turned bad?"

That would be the ultimate turn on. Watching Jess shed her innocence and go wild. With me. God, I could see it so clearly. I'd strip her naked. Lay her on my bed. Spread her legs. And go down on her. She'd taste divine. I'd lap and lick her until she screamed. Then I'd enter her. She'd be wet and tight. So tight...

Not. Going. To. Happen. Dickhead.

So I did the only thing I could. Pushed her away. Again.

"I like you as a friend, Jess, but that's it—"

"You're so full of it." She leaped to her feet so fast I got whiplash.

Rubbing my neck, I sat up, in time for her to shove me. "I'm sorry—"

"You can stick your apology up your ass." She towered over me, hands on hips, chest heaving. "I know what you think of me, Jack. Shy little virgin dabbling in a holiday fling so she can tell all her college buddies when she goes home."

She shook her head, but not before I glimpsed the sheen of tears. Fuck.

"But that's not me, and I thought you would've figured that out during the time we've spent together. As *friends*." She spat the last word as if it meant nothing. "Not that I think you know the meaning of the word, asshole."

I watched her storm out of my shack, torn between wanting to run after her and turning up the music again so I could drown out my thoughts. The main one being, I'd fucked up majorly and it was a good thing.

So why did I feel so goddamn bad?

15

JESS

I wanted to kill Jack.

Though I'd settle for maiming. Anything to inflict the same amount of pain he'd just put me through.

Every look, every touch, every word, implied that he liked me. Seriously liked me. As more than the 'friend' spiel he kept giving me. But he continued to push me away. And I knew why.

He had a major hang-up about our differences. To him, I was a good girl, the pristine little virgin he couldn't deflower.

Well screw that. And screw him.

If only I could...

"Hey, Jess." Chantal's heavily made-up face popped up on my laptop screen via Skype. "How's it hanging Down Under?"

"That sounds vaguely obscene," I said, an instant, vivid memory of Jack, naked, popping into my head.

My cousin waggled a finger at the screen. "Some of the hottest guys are in Australia and if you haven't had any action yet, I'll be seriously disappointed."

"You know me, Cuz. Not much to report."

Chantal wrinkled her nose. "That's what I was afraid of." She leaned closer to the screen. "Sweetie, when are you going to pop the cherry?"

I blushed. "Surely we've got more interesting things to talk about than my virginity?"

Chantal's smile faded. "Actually, there's something I want to talk to you about."

My cousin rarely looked serious. She sashayed through life, confident and bold. To see her concerned made me worry.

"What's up?"

She grimaced. "I hate to bring this up on your vacation, but you might like to know I checked with UNLV and that creep has transferred out. Already left the campus."

I sat up straighter. "That's great news."

The thought of not having to face Dave again at college was a huge relief. "Thanks for finding out and telling me."

"So you're not mad at me for poking around?"

"Mad? I'm freaking ecstatic." I blew her a kiss. "You're the best."

"I know." Chantal blew on her fingernails and polished them against her top. "So now that's out of the way, tell me if you've found a boy from OZ."

Not a boy. A man. A rugged, sexy, twenty-year-old, who wanted nothing more from me than friendship. Woop-de-freaking-do.

Chantal's eyes widened, her lash extensions almost touching her brows. "By your silence and that look, you've met someone. Tell all."

I mustered my best innocent expression. "No look here."

"There's a look." Chantal tilted her head to one side, studying me. "It's halfway between smug and excited and fearful. Which means there's a guy involved."

I sighed. Maybe articulating my confusion about Jack might help me deal with it. Because after the fun evening we'd just spent together, combined with the horse ride and bush picnic, I was confused. We clicked but was it one-sided and all in my imagination? Did he flirt like that with everyone and I'd misread it?

"There could be a guy. A guy who's freaking hot," I said in a rush. "Looks like Chris Hemsworth."

Chantal fanned her face and wolf whistled. "And?"

"And I really like him, and I think he likes me, but he keeps saying we can only be friends."

Chantal snorted. "Gay?"

"Uh…no."

"And you know this how?"

I felt the heat creeping into my cheeks. "Because I've seen the merchandise and it was pretty excited by me checking it out."

Chantal's jaw dropped. "You've seen the guy naked and he only wants to be friends? What's with that?"

"You tell me."

I valued Chantal's advice. My cousin knew guys. Could twist them around her little finger without trying. They took one look at her long legs and big boobs and shiny blonde hair and fell at her feet.

"The way I see it, the guy should be jumping your bones if he likes you. It's a perfect scenario. You're a holiday fling. Guys dig that. All the fun without the commitment."

I nodded. "That's what I thought but it's almost like…"

"What?"

At the risk of sounding like an idiot, I said, "It's like he thinks I'm too good for him or something. Like he doesn't want to take advantage of me."

Chantal's brow crinkled in consternation. "You didn't tell him you were a virgin, did you?"

I grimaced. "He kinda guessed."

"Girlfriend, there's your problem right there. You're nuts." Chantal made circular movements at her temple. "Some guys are put off by that, and maybe he spends all day in the outback breaking in horses and doesn't want to break you in."

I laughed. "He's not a horse wrangler."

"Well, it sounded nice in theory." Chantal grinned. "Honestly, Cuz? I have no idea what goes through guys' heads."

"That makes two of us."

"Maybe you should seduce him?"

I wrinkled my nose. "Not my style."

"If you want to get laid by the boy from OZ before you head home, maybe you should consider it." Chantal winked. "Always works for me."

I snorted. "Yeah, that's because you're blonde, have long legs, a great rack and dance at Burlesque Bombshells."

"You can do it, hun. I have full confidence in you." A doorbell sounded in the background and Chantal glanced over her shoulder. "Speaking of which, that's my date now." She blew me a kiss. "Later, gator."

"Have fun." I kissed my fingertips and pressed them to the screen, saddened when the screen faded to black.

I hadn't been homesick once since I'd arrived but chatting with Chantal made me yearn for the time when my life had been uncomplicated. Before Dave. Before Jack.

Though at least I could rest easy in the knowledge I

wouldn't have to face that jerk Dave when next semester started. Which only left one male complication in my life.

Jack.

What the hell should I do about Jack?

16

JACK

I hadn't slept all night.

I'd alternated between channel surfing and listening to my iPod. But hearing my favorite songs, the ones I'd danced to with Jess, had lost their appeal.

With the music blasting through the ear pieces and my eyes closed, all I could see was Jess dancing around my room; her hips swaying, her shoulders shimmying, her face radiant. Before our slow dance where it had taken every ounce of my dwindling willpower to not kiss her senseless and run my hands all over her body.

There'd been that *moment*, when I could've kissed her, that would haunt me for the rest of my life as a lesson in craving something so badly I could taste it, but reining in the urge to have it.

Discounting the physical torture, I'd genuinely had a great time with Jess. And then I'd had to deliberately ruin it.

I'd known I was in trouble the moment she'd chosen Dirty Dancing for us to watch. I'd lied. I had seen it. And I knew exactly why she'd chosen it. The whole good girl/bad boy theme, where Johnny and Baby get it on and everything worked out in the end? Pie in the sky stuff and the kind of romantic guff women loved.

I'd been so good, keeping my hands off her. But then the film had ended and we'd started verbally sparring again and the next thing I knew my head had been in her lap, her fingers were in my hair and she was telling me she wanted to be bad.

I'd had no choice. I had to push her away before we were both naked in five seconds flat and rolling around on the floor.

Jess deserved more.

She deserved one thousand thread sheets and roses and champagne and candles. She didn't deserve a quick fuck in a grungy outback shack to loud rock music.

"Thought I might find you out here." Reid clapped a hand on my back and I struggled not to flinch.

I'd never liked physical contact as a kid, had avoided it at all costs. The foster system bred a healthy distrust of touch in me, because the only times my foster folks or siblings had touched me was in backhanders or fisticuffs.

"Hey, mate. How was your trip?" I dumped the strawberries I'd picked into a basket and stuck out my hand.

"Good. Business went well." Reid shook it and I admired his strong handshake, despite his namby-pamby profession. "And I managed to see that restaurateur and chef I mentioned."

"Right," I muttered, trying not to sound too eager and hoping desperation didn't show on my face.

Reid laughed. "Don't go overboard with your enthusiasm."

I managed a wry grin. "So what did he say?"

"He said if the food you cook half lives up to my glowing recommendations, then he'd be lucky to have you." Reid slapped me on the back again. "So what do you say? Ready to move to Sydney and be apprenticed to a renowned chef?"

I couldn't speak. I wanted to but the words got stuck in my throat.

No one had ever done anything like this for me before and I had no idea how to begin to express my gratitude.

"Mate, I don't know what to say..." I cleared my throat and tried again. "Screw that. I do know what to say and it's a hell yeah."

"Great. Is a month long enough to give notice here and move down to Sydney?"

Completely overwhelmed by Reid's generosity, I shook my head. "Shouldn't be a problem."

In the past, I'd give the station owners a week's notice if that, moving on when the whim took me. But Doreen and Mrs. Gee had been good to me and I didn't want to leave them in the lurch. A month would be plenty. And would see out Jess's holiday here. Not that I should be registering a fact like that. Especially not now.

Because if I'd been determined to keep my hands off her before, my incentive had just doubled.

Reid Harper was a stand-up guy who'd just done me a massive favor. No way could I repay him by fucking his sister.

"Thanks again, mate." I pumped Reid's hand until mine almost fell off.

"As you Aussies say, no worries." Reid glanced at his

watch. "I've got a conference call happening in five minutes, so I'll give you all the details later."

"Sure, thanks."

I managed to wait until Reid rounded the front verandah and I heard the slam of the front door before letting out a resounding yell that would've startled the cattle all the way in the top paddock.

I had a chance at a fresh start. A real future. Far removed from my current drifter lifestyle that was growing old fast.

It was just the change I'd been looking for.

And the damndest thing, Jess was the first person I wanted to share the good news with.

17

JESS

"I hear congratulations are in order." I propped on the top rail of the fence, deliberately letting my skirt ride up. Let the moron see what he was missing out on.

Jack barely glanced up from weeding the vegetable garden. "Yeah, your brother is one helluva guy."

"I guess." When the uncomfortable silence grew—not surprising, considering last time I'd seen him I'd called him an asshole—I tried to make small talk. "Looking forward to living in Sydney?"

"Yeah."

Great. Monosyllabic answers and he wasn't looking at me. I didn't want to apologize because I'd meant every word I'd said at his place the other night, but I missed his teasing, missed us. Even if technically there wasn't an 'us'.

No matter what he said, we'd developed a bond. A

friendship. A connection. That he'd cheapened by implying I was just out for a holiday fling.

"I'm sorry about the other night," I blurted, sliding off the fence to land on my feet. "You're not an asshole."

"Yeah, I am, and you don't need to apologize." He finally glanced up, his expression wary. "I like you, Jess. I've never had a girl-friend before and it's been fun hanging out with you. But that's as far as it goes."

I didn't want to argue with him but I could feel my anger rising at his holier-than-thou speech. "Why do you get to make all the decisions in our relationship?"

"Relationship? Seriously?" He stood and swiped his grimy hands down the side of his jeans. "How did we go from friends to a relationship?"

"A friendship is a relationship, dumbass," I muttered, glaring at him, which is why I saw the exact moment is mouth switched from rebellious to amusement.

"Do you call all your friends names or is it just me?"

"It's you, Cookie." I deliberately used his nickname, knowing he liked it. "In case you were in any doubt, you're also a pain in the ass."

"Nice," he said, his wry grin making my heart do that weird flip flop thing it always did when he smiled. "Guess I won't tell you about the surprise I've organized then."

"Surprise?"

I immediately envisaged the two of us strolling off into an outback sunset, before REALITY CHECK flashed across my mind.

"Actually, I can't take all the credit. Mrs. Gee and Doreen suggested it."

Yep, there went my little fantasy of Jack and I alone together.

I studied my nails, feigning disinterest. "So, are you going to tell me some time this century?"

He laughed, a low, sexy sound that rippled over me and made my stomach free fall. "Fancy outback camping for a night?" He gestured at the sky. "Nothing like the sunrises in this part of the world."

Sunrises, right. Because all I could think about was the two of us sleeping side by side in a tent in the outback. Alone.

Did the guy want to torture me to death?

"So what do you say?" He winked. "Fancy spending your last night in OZ under the stars?"

"Uh, yeah, sounds good," I said, needing clarification. "So it'd be you and me?"

"And Reid." He made it sound so logical, that I shouldn't for one moment have jumped to the wrong conclusion that this would be a special trip for two. "It'll be great for you guys to have a real outback experience before you head home."

As opposed to the fake outback experience I was living, where a hot guy I really liked—and who liked me back— pretended that we were nothing more than friends.

"Thanks, sounds great." I tried to inject enthusiasm into my voice but he must've picked up on something, because he frowned.

"You don't like camping?"

"It's not that," I said, knowing I could never explain the reason behind my disappointment.

"Then what is it?"

I looked into his eyes, their striking green-blue highlighted by his tan, and wished with all my heart things could be different.

I'd been an idiot. I'd spent the last six days sulking after storming out of his shack, a small part of me hoping my absence would make his heart grow fonder.

So I'd wasted almost a week of our time together, time I could've spent hanging out with him, having fun. Instead, I'd plotted a million different scenarios in my head, ranging from slipping into his bed naked at night to storming his dusk shower.

But who was I kidding? I'd never have the guts to do anything like that. And I'd felt like a bitch, not congratulating him the moment Reid had returned with his offer.

The fact was, I couldn't deal with all the feelings making me go a little crazy. I'd never been in love. Wouldn't have a clue what it felt like. But this constant being on edge/thinking about him/craving him thing I had going on? Could be classed as a naive, clueless moron falling in love with someone who would never return the sentiment.

"Jess, what's wrong?"

I blinked, stared him straight in the eye, and lied. "Nothing. Thanks for inviting us to go camping. Should be a blast."

I bolted for the homestead before I told him the truth.

That I was crazy about him, the kind of crazy that extended to me giving up my life in America to share his in Australia if he asked.

18

JACK

"Sorry kids, I can't come." Reid slung his arms over my shoulder and Jess's. "Conference call with my boss and a hotshot from the cattle council tonight that I can't get out of. But you two go and have fun."

If I didn't already feel like a bastard for having constant lascivious thoughts about Jess, knowing that Reid trusted me to take his little sister camping made me feel worse.

"You're a workaholic, mate." I elbowed him and he grunted. "Sure you can't get out of it?"

Reid shook his head, while Jess stared at me with wide brown eyes. Was that a flicker of triumph I glimpsed?

"No can do. Politicians never sleep." Reid fake-knuckled his eyes.

"Yeah, that's because they're too busy sucking up to people." Jess smirked.

"Easy, Sis, or I'll ground you and stop you from going

camping." Reid bumped Jess with his hip and I envied their closeness. The Harpers were genuinely nice people and for a guy like me who rarely established ties with anyone, I'd miss them.

"*You* ground *me?*" Jess snorted. "Like to see you try." She elbowed Reid from the other side and he let out another grunt. "What time are we leaving, Jack?"

"In thirty minutes," I said, the beef pie and pumpkin scones I'd consumed for afternoon tea churning in my gut.

I needed that much time to weasel my way out of this camping caper, because no way was I spending a night under the stars with Jess. Alone.

"Okay, I'll meet you back here then." She practically skipped into the homestead and if I didn't know any better, I'd almost say she'd planned this.

Not that she could've, considering Reid's boss needed him to work, but did she have to look so damn chipper about it?

Her overt enthusiasm sparked an idea...I knew just how to get out of this.

"Reid, you're one of the most upfront blokes I've ever met, and you've done me a huge favor in securing that apprenticeship for me, so I think you should know—"

"My sister has a crush on you." Reid chuckled. "It's pretty obvious."

"Really?" I swallowed my trepidation, hoping my reciprocal crush wasn't quite so noticeable. "And you're okay with me taking her camping alone?"

Reid nodded. "'Course. You looked out for her while I was away and I trust you." He mock frowned. "Unless there's some reason I shouldn't?"

Damn, so much for getting out of this. Having Reid's

approval once he knew of Jess's feelings wasn't something I'd banked on.

"I'll look after her," I said, worrying about just how well I'd like to look after her.

"Good man." Reid hesitated, as if he wanted to say more and wasn't sure how to approach it. "Jess is an amazing kid. She lived in Craye Canyon with Mom until she got accepted into UNLV and has always done the right thing. I sometimes wish..."

"What?"

Reid blinked, as if caught up in memories. "That she'd step out of her comfort zone a little. Shake things up. Take risks. How do we learn unless we make mistakes?"

If that were the case, I'd be a frigging genius, I'd made so many of them.

"She's a nice girl," I said, hating how trite that massive understatement sounded.

Jess wasn't just nice. She was amazing. Sweet and sexy, fire and ice, sassy and cool.

I'd give my left ball to have one debauched night with her.

"Anyway, thanks again for taking her camping, Jack." Reid stared off in the distance. "Can't believe we leave tomorrow. This place has felt like a real home away from home. I'll miss it."

And I'd miss Jess.

The thought of not seeing her every day, even when she was strutting around with her nose in the air pretending to ignore me, made me sadder than I could've imagined.

I'd never grown attached to any woman. Ever. Mum abandoning me had seen to that. But the inexplicable bond I shared with Jess? Something I would definitely miss.

"We'll be back late morning, plenty of time to reach Cairns for your evening flight to Brisbane."

Reid grimaced. "Followed by a fifteen hour flight to LA with Jess snoring like a grizzly the whole way."

I laughed, wondering if I'd get the opportunity to hear Jess snoring tonight, and wishing I wasn't so damn happy by the prospect.

Reid shook my hand. "Thanks. I'll head in and rustle up Jess."

"No worries."

But as Reid headed into the homestead and I hoisted my swag onto my shoulder, I knew that spending the night under the stars with Jess would give me plenty to worry about.

19

JESS

I couldn't stop grinning.

For the entire hour on horseback that it took us to reach our camping destination, I smiled like an idiot.

I was finally spending the night with Jack.

Okay, so it wasn't quite the dream scenario, sleeping on hard ground with the possibility of Australia's deadliest creepy crawlies attacking me in my sleep. But with a little luck Jack would feel compelled to slip into my sleeping bag to protect me.

"I'll take care of the horses if you want to find kindling for a fire," he said, looking absolutely delectable as he took off his Akubra hat and ran a hand through his hair.

The simple action pulled his olive T-shirt tight across his chest, highlighting ridges of muscles I'd already seen. And wanted to see again.

He caught me staring but rather than looking away, I

raised an eyebrow in a silent dare. I had no idea how long our gazes locked, hot and challenging, before he turned away, giving me ample time to fan my face.

With one, scorching look, Jack had me hot and bothered. Incredibly hot.

Other girls in the dorm had vibrators. I'd seen them as their owners casually handed them around and discussed the pros and cons of different brands. Me? I used my hand, but that seemed pretty inadequate when confronted with Jack's blatant sexuality.

I wanted him.

I couldn't have him, in the story according to Jack.

Tonight, I really wanted to rewrite our ending.

"That fire won't start itself, you know," he flung over his shoulder and I sprung into action. I felt safe with Jack but I'd learned dusk fell quickly in these parts and I'd done enough research online to know I'd prefer a fire to keep the creepy crawlies at bay.

"Will it take long to set up the tent?"

He glanced at me, and my heart sank as I caught sight of his smirk. "What tent?"

"You're not serious?"

"Deadly." His smug grin widened, as if he knew my secret fear of Aussie fauna. "Why, nervous?"

"No," I lied, speeding up my kindling gathering. "So where do we sleep?"

"In sleeping bags with that for our roof." He pointed overhead, where I spotted the first smattering of stars. "I've done it a thousand times before. You'll be fine."

"Easy for you to say, Cookie. You don't have long hair that could house a nest of those red back spiders Doreen keeps mentioning."

His gaze drifted to my hair and an amazing thing

happened. His eyes blazed and his hands curled and unfurled, as if he wanted to run his hands through it.

"Plait it, and the sleeping bags have hoods." He turned away to resume tending the horses, but not before I'd seen a look of sheer longing. It snatched my breath. "Unless you want to chicken out now and head back?"

I was tempted. For all of two seconds, before I remembered this was my last night in Australia, my last night with Jack, and I wanted to make the most of it.

"No way," I said, bundling the kindling into my arms and dumping it in the clearing near our stuff. "Let's do this."

"That's my girl," he said, smiling his approval, and for a long, loaded moment I wished I was.

"You sure it's safe to camp out in the open?" I eyed the clearing dubiously. It seemed devoid of slithering nasties right now, but what about when darkness fell?

"I lied." He gave the horses a final pat, picked up his massive hiker's backpack and loped toward me. "I have a tiny two man tent in here."

"Idiot." I slugged him on the arm and he laughed.

"Was worth it to see your face." He pulled a horrified expression complete with goofy crossed eyes. *"Spiders might nest in my hair."* He mimicked me in a high falsetto that made me punch him again.

"Just for that, I'm going to find an ants' nest and leave a trail of honey direct to your sleeping bag," I said, trying to muster a defiant glare and failing because I was still laughing at his imitation of me.

"Did you pack honey?"

"No."

He smirked. "Well then, sweet thing, looks like you're out of luck."

"Smart ass," I muttered, as we shared a conspiratorial grin.

This is what I'd miss the most. Our camaraderie. When we hung out like this, teasing each other, I felt closer to Jack than I'd ever been to any other guy.

"I'm going to miss you," I blurted, instantly regretting my impulsive declaration when his smile faded and he raised the invisible barriers by deliberately blanking his expression.

"You don't even know me," he said, his tone devoid of emotion.

But I saw a vein pulsing in his neck as he swallowed; saw the glance away because he couldn't look me in the eye.

"I know you well enough," I said, determined to get us back onto easy footing, otherwise the rest of the night would be a bust. "I know you cook the best pasta outside of Italy. I know you like loud Aussie rock." I went for broke. "I know what you look like naked."

Heat flared in his expressive eyes as the backpack slipped from his hands to land at his feet. "Don't go there."

"Why not?" I tapped my bottom lip, pretending to think. "Though I do seem to have an unfair advantage. Because I've seen you naked and you haven't seen me."

He groaned. "You don't play fair."

"And you don't play at all."

I wish I was the kind of girl who had the courage to strip on the spot. The kind of girl to push the limits and see how Jack responded. But I'd never had that kind of chutzpah and it would be beyond humiliating if he still rejected me.

No way did I want my last memory of my time with Jack to be of him seeing me stark naked and still saying no.

"I better get this tent set up," he said, squatting to unzip the backpack.

"Chicken," I muttered under my breath, not sure if I was referring to him or me.

As I busied myself ensuring the firewood was in a neat pile to start the fire, Jack said in a low voice, "For what it's worth, I have seen you naked. In my fantasies all day and night."

I spun around so fast I stumbled and landed on my butt, sending the kindling scattering. "If you laugh, you're a dead man."

Jack's guffaws could've been heard back at the homestead, they were that loud, and I soon joined in. Every time one of us tried to stop, the other would start, until I held my side because of a massive stitch.

When he reached out his hand to me, I took it. He helped me to my feet. "You okay?"

"Yeah," I said, holding my breath the longer he held my hand. "Did you mean it? You've been fantasizing about me?"

He hesitated, then squeezed my hand before releasing it. I knew the exact moment our closeness vanished because he blinked, erasing the tenderness, replacing it with a harder edge. "Don't take it personally. It's a guy thing. We all do it. Pays to stock up the wank tank."

"The what?"

"It's like watching porn." He tapped his temple. "We stock up on naughty stuff up here for when we...you know." He mimicked masturbating and damn, if I wasn't turned on.

"Wank tank..." I let the words roll of my tongue, enjoying his tortured expression. "Must remember that for when I get down to business."

He spun on his heel and stalked away. "Fuck, Jess, I can't talk about this with you."

I had him rattled. Good. I wanted to see how far I could

push him. "Why not? We all get horny. We all need to get off. It's natural."

"Stop. Please." When he turned around, I saw the bulge in the front of his jeans, and grinned.

"Glad to see I'm not the only one who's turned on," I said, deliberately turning my back and walking toward the edge of the clearing.

I wanted him to come after me.

I willed him to come after me.

Instead, I heard him cursing as he resumed tent-erecting duties.

Not to worry.

The night was young.

20

JACK

I was in hell.

Squashed into a two-man tent, lying next to Jess, our sleeping bags touching but not being able to touch her.

Frigging blue ball hell.

I stared at the stars visible through our tent flap. Knowing it was futile making a wish on one but doing it anyway.

Whoever's up there, please give me the strength to get through this night without giving in to my instincts and fucking Jess senseless.

I adjusted my hard cock for the hundredth time since we'd crawled into our bags, wishing we'd packed up and headed home when we had the chance.

"It's beautiful," she murmured and I rolled onto my side to find her staring at me. "The sky."

I didn't need the clarification but I was grateful for it. Because if Jess kept staring at me like I'd hung every damn one of those stars, I'd lose it for sure.

"Go to sleep. We've got an early start if you want to see the sunrise."

"I'm too edgy to sleep." Her lips curved into a wicked smile that had me biting back a groan. "Do you know what helps me fall asleep back home?"

"You better say hot chocolate or chamomile tea or a handful of Valerian," I said, not liking where she was going with this.

She'd taunted me enough earlier, casually talking about getting off. I'd been hard ever since.

She smirked. "Orgasm is much more effective."

Fuck.

"I'm not doing this, Jess—"

"We're just making pillow talk," she said, her shadowed expression positively impish.

"Not any more." I turned away, unable to face her one moment longer without closing the short distance between us, and crushing her mouth with mine to shut her up.

"Fine. Have it your way." I didn't like her saucy tone. "But it's much more fun when another person's involved."

She wouldn't.

She couldn't.

Then I heard the rustle of her sleeping bag, the rhythmic movement of her hand rubbing against the lining, punctuated by her accelerated breathing and soft pants.

She was.

Jess was fucking masturbating. And making me listen.

So I gritted my teeth and did the only thing possible. Freed my cock, wrapped my hand around it and started stroking.

And damned if it wasn't the sexiest thing I'd done with a woman in a long time.

If Jess was trying to be quiet, she wasn't succeeding. Because I heard every gasp, every moan. Or maybe that was the point: she was trying to torture me. Or get me to give in and have sex with her.

But that wasn't going to happen. I'd told Reid I'd look after her and I would, even if my balls fell off in frustration.

I heard the exact moment she came, because she held her breath, before exhaling on a long, satisfied sigh.

And I stopped. I couldn't come inside my sleeping bag and jacking off lost its appeal when an unexpected sadness seeped through me.

I should've been the one bringing Jess to orgasm.

I should've swallowed her pants with long, hot, moist, open-mouthed kisses.

I should've sucked her tits while fingering her clit.

I should've gone down on her until she screamed.

I should've been her first.

But changing my life meant sticking to my new principles, even it meant lying here all frigging night, frustrated as hell and wishing things between us could be different.

∽

I MUST'VE EVENTUALLY DRIFTED off around three because I woke at five thirty with the pale dawn streaking the sky, to find my arm cuddling Jess and her head snuggled into my shoulder.

We had sleeping bags between us but I still got a boner. I could blame it on the usual morning woody but this one was a hell of a lot more painful and it had to do with the woman I'd wanted all damn night and couldn't have.

Her hair tickled my nostrils and I eased away slightly, not wanting to wake her just yet, wanting to savor our closeness.

I'd never get another chance to have her in my arms like this. I intended on making every second count.

I nuzzled her neck, inhaling her soft lilac fragrance. God, it was so evocative. So Jess. Sweet and elegant. Subtly sexy. I wanted her more than ever.

I allowed myself the luxury of brushing a feather-light kiss on her ear, her temple, her forehead. I daren't go near her lips for fear I'd never stop.

She moaned and wriggled, snuggling in deeper. It should've been my cue to remove my arm and move away. I didn't.

Her eyelids fluttered open, her beautiful brown eyes hazy and unfocussed. It took a few seconds for her to awaken fully and when she did, the smile that curved her lips was breathtaking.

"Good morning."

"It is now," I said, sounding incredibly corny but wanting to make this moment last.

She chuckled. "Sleep well?"

"Not as well as you."

If she registered my innuendo, she didn't show it. "Must be the fresh outback air."

"Must be," I said, remembering the sounds she made as she came last night, knowing I'd never forget as long as I lived.

"We're awfully cozy." She shrugged her shoulder where my arm currently resided. "Aren't you afraid I might ravish you or something?"

"Or something." I gave her a quick hug. "It's kinda nice waking up next to you like this."

"Yeah, it is." She smiled, but I saw her lower lip wobble. Fuck, I couldn't make her cry.

"The sun should be up in five minutes. You don't want to miss it—"

"Jack?"

"Yeah?"

"We can do a lot in five minutes."

I saw the blatant yearning in her eyes; saw how much she wanted me. And it made me feel ten feet tall that an amazing girl like her wanted me to be her first.

But if I'd managed to keep my hands off her all night, no frigging way would I make her first time a quick fuck before she flew back to the States this afternoon.

So I removed my arm with regret and unzipped my bag. "Yeah. Five minutes gives us enough time to get up, use the bush toilet and get ready to watch the most amazing sunrise you'll ever see."

Disappointment clouded her eyes as she turned away to unzip her bag. "Meet you outside," she said, her tone forlorn, and I curled my hands into fists to stop from reaching for her.

As I squeezed through the tent flaps and trudged outside, I swore walking away from her right then was the hardest thing I'd ever had to do.

21

JESS

So last night didn't live up to expectations.

I was still a virgin. A frustrated virgin.

On the upside? I'd had the most intense orgasm of my life.

Because I knew Jack had been listening.

I'd done it on purpose, hoping to drive him insane. Hoping he'd give in to the obvious attraction sizzling between us and finally have sex with me. But the guy had the willpower of a saint.

Worse? I'd woken to find him cuddling me, the tenderness in his eyes almost making me bawl.

So he liked me. Really liked me. But because of some misplaced chivalry he wouldn't touch me. If only we had more time together. If only I didn't have to fly home today.

The moment I thought it, the solution flickered to life again...

I could stay.

I'd contemplated it a few times, before dismissing it as a clingy act of desperation.

Absolute insanity, giving up my life back home to stay in Australia on a whim, but I could do it. If Jack wanted me to. And what was the likelihood of that?

"Idiot," I muttered, grabbing a roll of toilet paper and heading off to find a private spot in the bush. After the requisite scanning of the surrounding area for any animals/reptiles/bugs that could bite my ass, I quickly finished my business, used the sanitary hand lotion and headed back to camp, to find Jack had already dismantled the tent and packed everything away.

So much for him wanting me to stick around. He couldn't wait to get back to the homestead so I could leave for good.

"Come on. We've got a five minute walk to reach the best spot to watch the sun rise." He held out his hand and I didn't hesitate. I slipped my hand into his, relishing the contact.

I was such a sucker. Guess this was what love did to a girl.

Love?

I didn't love Jack. I couldn't.

Shit.

What if I did?

I blamed the sudden nausea on the fact I hadn't had any breakfast yet, but as we stopped at a rocky outcrop overlooking burnished copper plains as far as I could see, I knew my queasiness had more to do with the realization I'd fallen in love for the first time, with a guy who lived a world away.

"The perfect vantage point." He tugged me down and we sat cross-legged, side by side, as the sun peeped over the horizon. "I discovered this place by accident a few months ago, when I first arrived."

"It's beautiful," I said, staring at his profile and not the sun.

"I've come out here a few times, to clear my head."

I watched the tension bracketing his mouth soften as the sun continued to creep into the sky, bathing us in a breathtaking mauve, gold and sienna kaleidoscope.

"Don't you ever get lonely, doing stuff like this on your own?"

He glanced at me, a puzzled frown creasing his brow. "I like my independence. I learned pretty early on to depend on no one but myself." He paused, and his frown cleared. "But I have to say, having you with me, has made this time pretty special."

"I knew you liked me," I said, halfway between teasing and triumphant.

"'Course I like you."

I only just caught his muttered, "Too much for my own good."

"Shame we can't do something about it."

There, I said it. Put it out there. A blatant hint that I'd be willing to do whatever it took for us to be together.

He stared at me for a long, interminable moment, the sun's rays reflecting off his hair and creating a blond halo, illuminating his handsome face.

"No point wishing for things to be different when we can't change facts." He squeezed my hand and released it. "We need to look to the future. No regrets."

No regrets? Seriously? My heart was almost bursting with them, the main one being I'd never see him again after today.

He stood, brushed off his butt and walked away, leaving

me pressing the pads of my fingers to my eyes to stop from bawling, and cursing myself for being such a fool.

∽

WE'D BARELY SPOKEN on the ride back to Cooweer. Which was fine with me, because every time I glanced at Jack my chest ached.

The hour ride had been over too soon and while he tended to the horses, I paced outside his shack, alternating between scuffing my boots in the dirt and kicking up little tornadoes of dust, and glancing at the darkening sky.

Huge storm clouds had chased us all the way back to the homestead. With a little luck, a rare deluge for this time of year in these parts would cause a flood and keep me stranded here indefinitely.

Yeah, right, and I still believed in fairytales too.

Jack appeared around the far corner of the shack, near that fateful outdoor shower, as the first drops of rain plopped onto my nose.

"You better make it to the homestead before this hits," he said, barely breaking stride as he headed for the shack's front door.

"Still eager to get rid of me right to the very end, huh?" I kicked the dirt one last time, almost grateful for the sting of pain as I stubbed my big toe. It might detract from the massive pain breaking my heart in two.

"Just go, Jess." He ran a hand over his face, as if he couldn't stand the sight of me any longer, and that's when I finally lost it.

I'd put up with his hot and cold attitude for a month. The flirting. The teasing. Always followed by the withdrawal.

He'd made me fall in love with him without trying.

He liked me, but he couldn't have me.

Well screw him.

"Must be damn difficult, living a lie."

He paused on the top step. "What are you talking about?"

"You're a liar. Pretending like there's nothing going on between us. Pretending like you won't touch me for my own good. But want to know what I think?"

The rain fell heavier, soaking me to the skin. I didn't care. I didn't care about anything but getting this huge weight off my chest.

Because quiet, obedient, dutiful Jess Harper never spoke up. I held my tongue in any uncomfortable situation. I hated confrontation and would do anything to keep the peace.

Not this time. No way in hell would I spend a fifteen-hour flight back to LA lamenting the fact I didn't speak up when I had the chance.

"This is a waste of time, Jess. I'm doing this to protect you from me—"

"Shut the fuck up." I marched toward him as the heavens opened up and I had to shout to be heard. "I've done the right thing my entire life. I deliberately fade into the background. And I damn well don't tell a guy like you what I really think. But I'm leaving today so here goes nothing."

I jabbed my finger in his direction. "You're a wimp. A big, fat wuss who hides behind pathetic excuses because you're too damn scared to take a chance on what you feel in here."

I placed a hand over my heart. "I pity you, Jack, because you're an amazing guy and if you saw what I see in you, we could be incredible together—"

I never got to finish my sentence as he vaulted the steps,

landed at my feet, hauled me into his arms and slammed his mouth onto mine.

I saw stars. Literally. Because his kiss deprived me of oxygen. I couldn't breathe. Couldn't think. Couldn't comprehend that what I'd yearned for all this time was finally happening.

His tongue demanded entrance into my mouth and I let him in, our tongues dueling and tangling in a long, hot, open-mouthed kiss that defied belief.

His hands were everywhere. Grabbing my ass. Caressing my back. Delving into my hair. Palming my breasts.

Then he tweaked my nipples and I moaned, savoring the electric sensations shooting lower, where I throbbed with wanting him.

We didn't come up for air as Jack spun me around so my back was pressed against the shack wall, his kisses deepening as he ground his pelvis against me.

I hoisted a leg around his waist, craving deeper contact. Craving him inside me.

I arched against him and he groaned, a guttural, sexy sound that empowered me as a woman.

Jack wanted me. Really wanted me. It made me braver than I'd ever been with any guy.

I stroked his back, relishing the hard muscles beneath my palms. My fingertips skimmed the skin between his T-shirt and jeans. It was smooth and wet and I wanted more.

And that's when I made a fatal mistake.

I slid my fingers beneath his waistband. Eased my hips away so I could slide my hands around the front to touch him...

He wrenched his mouth off mine and pulled away so fast I stumbled.

"Fuck, that never should've happened." He stared at me

in wild-eyed horror, as if we'd done something wrong, and the last of my patience snapped.

"Bullshit. That's the kiss that should've happened weeks ago if you had any balls." I shoved him away, hard, my hands curling into fists, wanting to lash out and pummel him until he hurt as badly as I did. "I hope you relive it every fucking night for the rest of your life and think about what else you missed out on."

I pushed past him and ran, blinded by the rain but grateful the downpour camouflaged the tears cascading down my cheeks.

22

JACK

I was numb.

Physically. Emotionally. I couldn't feel a thing as I trudged inside. I mechanically peeled off my wet T-shirt, jeans and jocks, and toweled off.

Jess had gone.

And I'd ended things between us in the worst possible way.

I'd mulled long and hard during the hour-long return journey to Cooweer. I'd been a prick for weeks, alternating between flirting and pushing her away. Wasn't her fault I'd grown a conscience at the ripe old age of twenty.

My recent choices to lead a better life had inadvertently affected her, so I'd wanted to do things right. I'd planned on writing everything down in a letter and giving it to her to read later. That way, if she wanted to keep in touch like I planned on doing with Reid, it would be her choice.

But I'd shot that to shit by finally giving in to my baser instincts and kissing her.

Fuck, it had been the best damn kiss of my life.

Sweet and sensual and so damn erotic I was still hard.

And the fallout would be catastrophic, because I'd never be able to get her out of my head now.

I wanted more. I wanted all of her.

So I settled for doing whatever I could to rectify the shitty situation I'd created.

I pulled on sweatpants, grabbed the pen and notepad I used to jot down recipes when I brainstormed, and sat on the couch.

School hadn't been high on my list of priorities as a kid and shifting around between foster families ensured I didn't stay in one place long enough to build a solid education. So the fact I wanted to make the effort to write to Jess showed just how much she meant to me.

I chewed the end of the pen and stared at the blank paper, willing my jumbled thoughts to coalesce into something that would make sense. But the harder I focused the more the words in my head scrambled, so I settled for being blunt and writing exactly how I felt.

DEAR JESS,

I'm sorry I screwed up so bad. You were right. I'm shit scared by how you make me feel. Confused and terrified, yet happy. I've never been happier than this past month, when we've hung out together. You make me laugh. And you've got a smart mouth, one that I finally got to kiss today.

God, you have no idea how badly I've wanted to do that. And more. Because despite pushing you away, mostly for your own good, I've wanted to be your first lover. That night in the tent? I heard you and I wanted to be the one to finger your clit. To go down on you. To lick you until you screamed my name. I wanted to slide my hard cock inside you and fuck you all night long.

But I made a choice not long before you arrived that I wouldn't be that guy anymore. The kind of guy who has casual sex and seeks short-term solutions without thought for the future.

Thanks to your brother, I now have a future. I'm going to do my apprenticeship. Get my own restaurant one day. Make him proud of me. And make me proud of me.

Because that's the thing, Jess. I've always felt like a loser. I've been told it often enough growing up and after I while, guess I started to believe it. I've spent the last few years running. Running from my past. Running from my own insecurities.

But I finally took a stand recently and unfortunately, you've borne the brunt of it.

Me not sleeping with you has got nothing to do with how desirable you are as a woman or how naive. You're a huge turn on, Jess. Huge. I want you so much you make me ache. This has all been about me, not you.

I don't believe in making promises or dreaming the impossible dream. But know this.

I'll never forget you, Jess.

Ever.

And who knows, one day you may stroll into a Sydney restaurant and want to give the chef your compliments with a kiss reminiscent of the one we shared today.

You're the most incredible woman I've ever met.

Love always,

Jack xx

I REREAD the letter and almost screwed it into a ball. It was crap. But it was from my heart and I wanted Jess to know the truth. She didn't deserve to be jerked around the way I'd done with her.

Feeling like a schmuck, I folded it carefully and slid it into my pocket. I'd give it to her just before she got in the car and tell her to wait until she had a private moment to read it. Last thing I wanted was Reid looking over her shoulder on the plane or worse, having to console her if she fell apart.

The letter crinkled in my pocket as I stood, a testament to the young woman who'd stolen my heart without trying.

23

JESS

I made it halfway to the homestead when the chills set in.

Not from being saturated, but from the realization that the last time I'd see Jack alone before I left was that confrontation where I'd acted like a lunatic.

The fact he'd kissed me, when he'd gone to great lengths over the last four weeks not to, meant he cared. And while I wasn't stupid enough to believe in long distance relationships, the fact he'd become good friends with Reid meant the guys would stay in touch. So who knew what the future held?

But for us to have any chance, even maintaining a friendship, I had to go back.

I had to behave like a rational, mature woman, not a slighted almost-nineteen year old that threw a tantrum when she didn't get what she wanted.

Because that's how I'd pretty much behaved during my entire stay. Pushing him. Taunting him. Abusing him when he didn't reciprocate the way I wanted. Then ignoring him.

And I sure as hell didn't want his last memory of me to be a screaming banshee who shoved him away.

So I turned around and headed back.

The rain hadn't eased. It poured down in diagonal sheets, soaking everything in its path. I dragged my feet through the mud, clueless as to what I'd say when I reached the shack. The spontaneity thing hadn't worked so well for me with Jack up to this point.

As the shack came into sight, the rain eased and the sun poked out from behind a cloud, making the grungy corrugated iron almost gleam.

The place looked welcoming, despite its forlorn exterior. And even now, I'd give anything to stay.

That's what I'd tell him.

The truth.

It was as easy as that. No use trying to make excuses for my behavior. I'd tell him exactly how I felt. I'd already behaved like an idiot. What did I have to lose?

I skipped up the steps, knocked twice, before turning the doorknob and flinging the door open.

Jack, in the process of scrolling through his iPod, gaped at me.

"I had to come back. I'm sorry for before. For behaving like a spoilt brat these last few weeks." I pressed my hands to my chest. Yeah, like that would stop my heart from leaping out. "The truth is I've fallen in love with you. And I'd give up everything to stay with you if you asked me."

I blurted it all out in a rush, the words tumbling over each other. I had to say it fast because if I didn't, I'd second-guess the wisdom of handing him my heart on a platter with one hand and a knife in the other.

Jack stared at me, his eyes like steely lasers, boring into me, cutting deep.

He didn't make a move toward me. He didn't smile. He didn't hold out his arms.

And I knew the devastating truth before he opened his mouth to speak.

"Jess, you're a teenager. You'll fall in love many times before you find the right guy." He squared his shoulders and shook his head. "You have a crush and it's naive to build it up into anything more than that."

I began to shake as shock set in and rather than rush over to comfort me, Jack thrust his hands into his pockets. He faltered, his stoic expression crumpling a little as he half pulled out a folded piece of paper.

He stared at it for a few, interminable seconds before finally dragging his gaze away to look me in the eye.

"Bye, Jess. I hope you find what you're looking for."

Then he strode past me, out the door, and out of my life.

24

JACK

To Mrs. Gee's credit, she stayed clear of me as I moved through the kitchen like a madman. Pummeling dough. Hammering steaks. Kneading bread until every joint in my hands ached.

But it was nothing on the ache in my chest.

Jess loved me.

Loved me so much she'd give up her entire life to stay if I asked her.

When she'd told me, my heart had stopped. I hadn't been able to breathe. I couldn't comprehend someone could care for me that much let alone want to give up everything to be with me.

I was a drifter bum with no ties to anyone or any place.

Jess was in her first year at uni with so many options.

I was blue collar. She was cashmere and pearls.

But none of that mattered to her and that's what

humbled me the most: that she saw past my tough outer shell and believed in the real me. The guy with hopes and dreams of making it big in the culinary world. The guy who secretly liked chick flicks. The guy who would give anything to have a girl like her by my side.

Yeah, I loved her too. Loved her so much I had to let her go.

No way would I be responsible for her giving up her dreams to follow mine on a whim. I had no idea what awaited me in Sydney. How long my savings would last with the exorbitant rental prices. What kind of hovel I'd need to live in while I worked manic hours at the restaurant.

Jess deserved better than that. Way better. The thought of her leaving her life, her family, behind for me, was unbearable.

Simply, I had nothing to offer her.

The best thing I could do for her was to let her explore the world on her own. Develop into her own person. And try my damndest to forget I'd passed up the opportunity of a lifetime, to have her with me.

"The Harpers are leaving." Mrs. Gee took the meat knife out of my hand. "Don't you want to say goodbye?"

"Already have," I grunted, willing my voice not to betray the utter devastation making me almost shake at not seeing Jess again.

Mrs. Gee tut-tutted. "Well, I'm going outside to see them off." She sent me a pointed glare. "It's only polite."

I waited until she shuffled out of the kitchen before I pulled the letter out of my pocket.

I couldn't go outside to farewell Jess without doing something first.

A pot of chicken chasseur simmered on the stove and I

stuck an edge of the letter into the burner, waited for it to catch, before heading for the sink.

As the letter flamed, I'm sure my heart cracked wide open, the pain was that bad.

When my fingers were in danger of being scorched, I dropped the remnants into the sink and watched it turn to ashes.

Ironic. The first and only time I'd ever been honest with a woman, I'd watched it go up in smoke.

If deliberately pushing Jess away had been the hardest thing I'd ever had to do, burning that letter had come a close second. And now I faced a third.

Saying goodbye in public to the woman I loved.

And pretending I didn't love her at all.

25

JESS

I said my goodbyes like an automaton. Mechanical. Stilted. Overly formal.

If anyone noticed, they didn't say. Then again, they could attribute it to my love of the outback and my reluctance to farewell this breathtaking country. Yeah, right.

"Ready to go, Sis?" Reid draped his arm across my shoulder.

"Yeah." I managed to keep my voice steady, glad the numbness that had set in around the time Jack had flung my declaration back in my face had filtered through to my vocal cords.

Even my voice sounded mechanical, almost tinny. It was better than the alternative. A wailing, blubbery mess.

Not that I'd cry again. I'd wasted enough tears on Jack McVeigh. No more.

Never again.

Of course, that's the moment he chose to saunter around the veranda corner, swiping his hands down the front of his apron.

My heart gave a traitorous jolt and when he looked at me, the familiar heat spread through me. Looked like my body hadn't got the memo my head dictated: FIRST CLASS PRICK. DELETE FROM MEMORY.

"Hey, there's Jack." Unfortunately, Reid didn't remove his arm from my shoulder when he all but dragged me across the short distance separating us. "Next time I see you, Jack, I'm expecting the best cordon bleu in Sydney."

"You're on, mate." Jack responded to Reid but it seemed he only had eyes for me. Eyes that I wanted to gouge out.

Reid shook Jack's hand, finally giving me the opportunity to slip out from under his other arm.

"Safe trip, guys." Jack managed a tight smile. "I have to get back to the kitchen."

"Sure thing." Reid did some dorky salute while I managed a mute nod.

I thought I'd got off easily, until Reid said, "Nothing to say, Jess? That's gotta be a first."

What could I say? That I'd fallen in love for the first time in my life...with a complete jackass?

That I'd laid my heart on the line and had it trampled by a bad boy who believed his own badass press?

That I'd been a total fool and even now, couldn't stop from locking gazes with Jack one last time in the hope... what? He'd actually admit to wanting me enough to ask me to stay? He'd apologize for breaking my heart? For belittling what we'd had by implying I was a naive teenager who'd mistaken a vacation crush for something more?

I searched his eyes for some sign, for some indication

that I was right and he was wrong. What I saw was sadness and regret.

I knew the feeling.

I swallowed the emotion welling in my throat. "Bye, Cookie. Have a good life."

"Ditto," Jack said, some of the tension around his mouth dissipating when I used my nickname for him.

"Wrong chick flick," I said, wondering if he'd get my reference to that night we spent dancing and watching a corny DVD and being totally in the moment.

"I'd take Ghost over Dirty Dancing any day," he said, some of the usual spark returning to his eyes.

"Not bad, considering they both star Patrick Swayze, but you know you've just admitted to watching two chick flicks?"

"Nothing wrong with being a metrosexual, right, Reid?"

I blinked, surprised to find my brother right next to me, his head swiveling between us as if watching a particularly interesting debate.

Reid laughed. "I'm an action guy so you've lost me." He nudged me. "Time to leave. You can watch all the chick flicks you like on the long flight home."

Hopefully it would take my mind off Jack and how, even now, after all we'd been through, after how much he'd hurt me, it didn't take much for us to revert to our lighthearted, teasing best.

"See you later." With one last, loaded stare in my direction that I had no hope of interpreting, Jack raised his hand in a wave and walked away.

My vow to not cry over him again? Sorely tested, as I said another hurried round of goodbyes to Doreen, Mrs. Gee and Gladys, before sliding into the four-wheel-drive's back seat.

As the car drove away, bumping along the potholed drive, I glanced back.

In time to see Jack pause at the kitchen door and raise his hand.

He couldn't see me at this distance but I did the same, feeling like some lovesick heroine out of a chick flick we both seemed to like, even if one of us—him—wouldn't admit.

Only when the car exited the main gate in a cloud of red dust did I lose sight of Jack and I finally lowered my hand.

As we drove away from Cooweer and I struggled not to bawl, one question plagued me.

What if I'd stayed anyway?

Want an exclusive bonus epilogue?

Want to read Jess and Jack's sizzling reunion?
Read BRASH, out now!

FREE BOOK AND MORE

SIGN UP TO NICOLA'S NEWSLETTER for a free book!

Try the **BOMBSHELLS** series

BEFORE (FREE!)

BRASH

BLUSH

BOLD

BAD

BOMBSHELLS BOXED SET

The **WORLD APART** series

WALKING THE LINE (FREE!)

CROSSING THE LINE

TOWING THE LINE

BLURRING THE LINE

WORLD APART BOXED SET

The **HOT ISLAND NIGHTS** duo

WICKED NIGHTS

WANTON NIGHTS

The **BOLLYWOOD BILLIONAIRES** series

FAKING IT

MAKING IT

The **LOOKING FOR LOVE** series

LUCKY LOVE

CRAZY LOVE

WRITING ROMANCE AS NIKKI NORTH

FREE IN KU

Read the '**MILLIONAIRE IN THE CITY**' series.

LUCKY

COCKY

CRAZY

FANCY

FLIRTY

FOLLY

MADLY

Check out the **ESCAPE WITH ME** series.

DATE ME

LOVE ME

DARE ME

TRUST ME

FORGIVE ME

Try the **LAW BREAKER** series
THE DEAL MAKER
THE CONTRACT BREAKER

And the **CREATIVE IN LOVE** series (releasing late 2021)
ALMOST YOURS
ALMOST MINE
ALMOST PERFECT

Check out Nicola's website for a full list of her books.

EXCERPT FROM BRASH

Chapter One

Jess Harper was the first to admit, sex made her uncomfortable.

Not the act itself, despite the lackluster efforts by her ex, but the paraphernalia that surrounded her every time she stepped into Burlesque Bombshell, her cousin's Vegas dance venue.

The nipple tassels and diamante thongs and shiny poles made her feel inadequate. Like all that overt sexiness screamed she was a failure in the boudoir. She wasn't. It was the dorks she allowed in there that needed lessons: Getting It On 101.

She pushed through a phalanx of fuchsia feather fans and slipped into the main dressing room, only to be confronted by nudity.

"Jeez, put some clothes on," she said, unable to resist brushing against the vermillion velvet walls as she entered. The plushness of this room never failed to bring out her inner vixen.

"Don't like the view? You know where the door is." Zazz, Burlesque Bombshell's premier dancer, leaned closer to the gilt edged, beveled mirror and puckered up, before slicking vivid crimson across her lips.

"Not a problem. But then who'd plan your gargantuan wedding, huh?" Jess picked up an armful of feather boas and draped them over a mannequin before slouching on a plush peacock blue suede daybed. "Wedding of the century, babe. Your quote, not mine."

"Whatever." Zazz batted her eyelash extensions and pouted. "Table arrangements finalized?"

"Yep. Ruby linen tablecloths. Matching chairs tied with black bows. Elongated glass vases filled with ebony crystals and long feathers. Silverware. Black candles. And bling name holders—"

"Whoa. Detail overload." Zazz held up her hands. "As long as it matches the pics of that swank London Goth wedding you showed me in a bridal mag, I'm happy."

"Easy to please." Jess used her hand as a fake notebook and jotted with an imaginary pen. "Not."

"You're snooty because I haven't told you the venue yet." Zazz sniggered. "Trust me, you're going to love it."

Jess didn't have to love it. In fact, she couldn't give a flying fig if the venue had rope swings hanging from the roof and chains from the chandeliers. The faster she was done doing this favor for her mom, who'd coerced her into planning this wedding from her sickbed, the faster she could figure out what she'd do with the rest of her life.

One thing Jess knew for sure; it wouldn't be helping Pam, her flamboyant mom, plan any more crazy weddings.

"And wait 'til you hear about the food." Zazz shrugged into an emerald satin kimono embroidered with topaz crystals. "Michelin starred. Exotic. To die for."

"Good. Faster I know about the cake, faster I can get onto the cake table decorations."

Zazz cinched the sash at her waist, accentuating her knockout hourglass figure. "The chef should be here shortly so you can sit down together and go over boring deets like which canapés go with which wines."

"Goody." Jess clapped her hands in fake excitement. Last thing she felt like doing today was collaborating with some temperamental, egotistical chef. Visiting her mom first thing had been bad enough. "Getting back to the venue. You know I can't finalize everything 'til I see the room, get a feel for the layout—"

"Relax. We're flying you and the chef out to the island end of the week."

"Island?" Jess's jaded soul couldn't help but perk up at the idea of a free trip to some exotic island. "Where?"

"Prince Island."

"Never heard of it." Not that Jess cared. Any place with island in the title? She was there with flip-flops on.

Zazz smirked. "That's because my darling fiancé owns the island. Six star resort and private villas. Totally exclusive. Invitation only."

Jess clutched her heart in mock shock. "Serious?"

Zazz laughed. "Yeah, who would've thought Dorian would be a romantic?"

Nothing the doting groom did would surprise Jess. Dorian Gibbs owned most of Nevada and ruled Vegas but held his coveted bachelorhood as the biggest prize. Until he'd attended a Bombshell soiree, taken one glimpse at Zazz and fallen head over heels.

Jess didn't believe in clichés but there was something undeniably electric when Dorian and Zazz were in the same room. Pity the odd lightning bolt or two couldn't strike her.

She could do with a good jumpstart. Her love life was on par with her career—down the toilet.

"Dorian would gift you the world on a silver platter if he could."

"I'm worth it." Zazz wriggled her fingers into a white satin glove and rolled it up to her elbow, smoothing it before repeating the elegant action on the other arm. "You are too, hun, and you'd know it if you'd ever let me fix you up with one of his friends."

"I prefer my guy to be in the same decade."

"Bitch." Zazz laughed. "Trust me, there's something to be said for an older man." She shimmied her hips, complete with a few crude pelvic thrusts. "They have the moves and know how to use them."

Jess winced. "If that's an indication of Dorian's moves, you can keep them."

"And relish them twice a day." Zazz propped on the end of her dresser and folded her arms. "Seriously, when's the last time you had a date?"

Jess opened her mouth to respond and Zazz rushed on, "One that didn't involve battery operated apparatus."

"I get out."

Zazz harrumphed. "Taking your mom to rehab doesn't count."

"She needs my help."

"She's had a stroke and is taking full advantage of the fact to have you at her beck and call." Zazz shook her head. "Don't get me wrong, I appreciate you stepping in to take over as my wedding planner. But Pam's milking this for all she's worth."

Didn't Jess know it. Sure, she felt sorry for her vibrant mom suffering a stroke that rendered her left side immobilized. And she didn't begrudge helping her. What she couldn't stand was the constant interference in her life when she'd escaped Pam's smothering years earlier.

They may live in Craye Canyon, an hour out of Vegas, but that's where the similarities between her life and her mom's ended.

Pam went through boyfriends like coffee filters. She pranced around town in mini skirts and tube tops, had her hair blow-waved daily and cleaned out the town's cosmetic supply on a regular basis. She planned weddings with panache and style, at odds with her loud, brash self.

Little wonder Jess had chosen an occupation far removed from her mom's flamboyance. Town librarian was staid, unassuming and quiet. It suited Jess just fine. Until she'd heard rumors the local council considered Craye Canyon Library a dead loss and would downsize soon, so she saved them the trouble and quit, leaving her jobless and directionless.

In a way, planning Zazz's wedding had given her breathing space to decide where she went from here. One thing Jess knew, she was tired of her boring life. Sick to death of it. Zazz was right. She needed to shake things up a little.

"You need an island fling." Zazz snapped her fingers, her grin positively evil. "Hot stud. Sun, surf, sex."

Sounded pretty damn perfect. "And here I was, thinking you were flying me to some island to plan your wedding."

Zazz waved away her concern. "It'll happen, I have full confidence in you."

"The wedding or the sex?"

"Both." Zazz's eyes narrowed as she smirked. "How do you like your eggs in the morning?"

"Huh?"

"The chef?" Zazz fanned her face. "Unbe-freaking-lievable. Sex on legs."

"Yeah, right." Jess rolled her eyes. "Those black and white checkered pants do it for me every time."

Zazz laughed. "Trust me, once you get a look at this guy, those ugly pants won't be staying on for long."

"Chefs aren't my type."

The moment the lie tumbled from Jess's lips, memories long suppressed flashed before her eyes.

An outback holiday in Australia. A cattle station cook. A kiss that defied belief. And a refusal that burned, real bad.

Jack McVeigh graced TV screens the world over these days, a constant reminder of what she'd once wanted and couldn't have. With that bad boy stubble, murky green eyes and lazy smile, no great surprise he'd won the hearts of viewers glued to his gourmet cooking show with the same ease he'd won hers.

Pity the celebrity chef preferred to break hearts along with eggs.

"Trust me, babe. If this chef can't get into your panties, no one will."

Unease rippled down Jess's spine like a premonition. "Who's this mystery guy?"

Zazz glanced at her watch. "You'll see for yourself in five minutes. I asked him to meet us here."

Jess ignored the persistent tingle that maybe, just maybe, Zazz's chef could be Jack.

Impossible, considering Jack was based in Sydney and had enough gigs to keep him busy into the next century. Yeah, she Googled him, so what?

Besides, Zazz had said the chef catering the wedding was an old friend of Dorian's so the guy had to be the same vintage.

She didn't know what bothered her more: the sliver of

disappointment she wouldn't see Jack face to face after a decade or the inhuman leap of her libido at the thought of a little one-on-one island time with the sexy chef.

"I need to check my final show times with Chantal." Zazz slipped her dainty feet into a pair of marabou feather mules and tightened the sash on her robe. "I'll be back in time for our meeting."

"What's his name—" Jess called out to Zazz's retreating back, wishing she had half the hip wiggle the sassy dancer had.

When Jess walked, men didn't stumble or gawk. She didn't warrant second glances or come-ons. She achieved exactly what she wanted to—anonymity and serenity, two qualities far removed from her boisterous, cringe-worthy mom.

With a sigh, she stood and wandered around the room, her fingertips stroking the satins and silks, savoring the lush fabrics she could never wear in a million years.

Her fingers snagged on a set of gold spangled pasties complete with sparkly-fringed tassels and she picked them up, held them over her nipples, and grimaced.

So not her.

"Hey Jess."

Shock ripped through the carefully constructed poise Jess had honed to a fine art over the years as her hands fell to her sides.

She'd envisaged her first meeting with Jack over the years. Kinda inevitable, with her brother Reid being his best mate.

In her scenarios, their first meeting after a decade didn't involve nipple pasties. Or a smoother-than-whisky voice that made her palms sweat, her skin prickle and her inner bombshell want to strip on the spot.

"Hey you."

Not quite the scintillating opening gambit she'd imagined. Then again, having this big, bronze Aussie cross the room to stand less than a foot away had thrown her brain into chaos and her body into meltdown.

"Nice tassels."

His fingertip toyed with the nipple tassels hanging limply in her hand and she stiffened.

In the past, she would've responded with a blush. But after what he'd done to her? The way he'd humiliated her? Not a chance in hell she'd give him the satisfaction of seeing her cave again.

She held them over her breasts, vindicated when those impossibly green eyes widened, the pupils constricting. "Care to see them on?"

He took a step back. "Don't play with fire."

She took a step forward. "Maybe I'm in the mood to get hot?"

He swore. "You and me? Not going to happen."

"So you've said before," she drawled, giving the tassels a twirl for good measure, reveling in his discomfort as he tore his gaze away from her breasts. "But a decade is a long time."

"Not frigging long enough," he muttered, casting a desperate glance at the door.

So she ramped up the tension.

"These?" She waved the tassels in his face, deliberately taunting. "Tip of the iceberg in my new wardrobe. You should see me in the purple suspenders and sheer, crotchless—"

"Enough." A low, warning growl she had no intention of obeying. "Is this the way you treated your fiancé? Not surprised he bolted."

Just like that, her bravado faded, replaced by the dogged insecurity that tainted her botched relationship with Max, and fury at Jack for judging her.

"Fuck you." She eyeballed him, willing away the incriminating tears stinging her eyes.

That's when she saw the glimmer of victory in his eyes and knew he'd deliberately insulted her to push her away, like he had ten years earlier.

He turned and headed for the door, but not before she heard his murmured, "Babe, you have no idea how much I wish for that."

Chapter Two

Jack wanted to punch something. Hard.

He settled for pacing the ridiculously narrow hallway backstage at Burlesque Bombshell.

The revue venue channeled a bordello with its crimson walls and filmy curtains and muted lights. And then there was Jess, standing in front of a mirror holding a pair of pasties to her nipples...

He stumbled and kicked out at a stray lead from a pink-fringed lamp tucked into a blind corner.

Wasn't Jess's fault he'd taken one look at her with those frigging pasties and imagined her modeling them, naked. He'd been hard in an instant, his cock's betraying response catapulting him back a decade when all he had to do was look at the naïve Yank to get a hard-on of crippling proportions.

Looked like nothing had changed.

He'd acted like a jerk to cover his reaction, to ensure she backed off before he did something stupid like haul her into his arms, back her up against the velvet wall and enter her.

She'd caught him off guard. His excuse, he was sticking to it. Anything to ease the guilt burning his gullet like acid at the hurt bewilderment he'd glimpsed in her expressive brown eyes.

He'd lashed out deliberately, an instinct that had served their tension-fraught relationship well during her one month vacation in outback OZ ten years ago.

For as much as he'd wanted the refined, softly spoken girl with the shy smile and steady stare, she'd been off-limits. Way out of his league.

He owed Reid Harper, big-time. No way would he screw up with Reid by screwing his sister.

So he'd lied. Pushed Jess away. Done everything he could to stop her hanging around him.

She hadn't listened. Somehow she'd seen through his act, had seen down to his soul sometimes. And they'd talked and laughed and eventually kissed.

It had been inevitable.

And wrong.

Now he had to march back into that barf-worthy frou-frou room and apologize. Because Reid had asked him to cater Dorian's wedding as a favor and Dorian had said he had to meet the wedding planner here today at five.

Which only added up to one thing. He'd be working with Jess to ensure this wedding went off without a hitch.

He pinched the bridge of his nose. It did little to alleviate the pressure building there. Along with Reid, Dorian had had a hand in launching his career into the stratosphere.

What Reid had seen in a lowly outback station cook he'd never know, but the guy had secured him an apprenticeship under a Michelin starred chef in Sydney and he hadn't looked back.

Dorian had been the first to invest in him too, with a

sizable financial chunk that enabled him to set up Cookie's, his own restaurant, and build a cult following.

Jack owed these two men everything.

He couldn't let them down.

Muttering a string of inventive curses under his breath, he squared his shoulders and marched back into the room.

To find Jess dabbing at her eyes with a tissue. That sight more than anything she'd said earlier hit him like a punch to the gut.

Feeling worse than a dry-mouthed and desperate blue-tongued lizard slinking through the Simpson Desert, he strode toward her.

"Jess, I'm really sorry—"

"Screw you." He admired her feistiness as she stared him down and flipped him the bird. "Newsflash. If you can't take a little heat, get out of the kitchen."

The corners of his mouth twitched. "You're using cooking puns to get rid of me?"

"I'll use anything I goddamn like to get rid of you," she said, a flash of fire darkening her eyes to ebony before she blinked and the telltale cool he remembered returned. "We can't work together."

He held up his hands in surrender. "You'll get no argument from me."

"Okay then." She nodded. "You leave, I'll invent an excuse, something along the lines of your rotten green peppercorn rib-eye gave the entire eastern seaboard of Australia food poisoning."

"Picking on my signature dish is harsh, don't you think?"

"No harsher than deliberately pushing away someone who cares about you."

Wow. She'd never been this outspoken back then. He liked the new sassiness. Very sexy.

Not helping the hard-on situation, dickhead.

"Why don't *you* leave? We're in Vegas. There's a wannabe wedding planner on every corner."

"I can't. Zazz trusts Chantal implicitly, and my cousin's from my hometown." She plucked at her sleeve cuff, a vulnerable tell he irrationally remembered. "Mom's the best wedding planner around but she's sick so I'm it."

"How's Pam doing?"

"Driving the physical therapists nuts at rehab. Bossing around the nurses. Making life hell for the doctors."

He laughed. "Reid said the same."

Her eyebrow rose slightly. "You guys still close?"

"We hang out when our schedules tee up."

"Because he never mentions you."

Duh. That's because Jack had made certain of it all those years ago, telling Reid about Jess's crush on him and how he didn't want it to affect their friendship.

Reid had respected him for it. While Jack had felt like a heel, lying to the guy who'd soon become his best mate.

For Jess's crush hadn't been one-sided. They'd had some serious chemistry. Their one explosive kiss had been testament to it.

Exactly why there could never be a repeat. Jack had spent his childhood and teen years making mistake after mistake, being shunted from one foster family to the next, being a screw up.

No way in hell would he stuff up the lifeline Reid Harper had offered him. Even if it included pushing away the one woman he'd ever let get close enough to seeing the real him.

"Guys aren't real big on chit chat," he said, gesturing for her to take a seat.

Standing this close, he could smell lilacs, the memories

of the way it had clung to his skin making him want to touch her so badly he ached.

"Yeah, so I've learned."

Her slumped shoulders made him want to shake the defeatist out of her and bring back the sass.

"I presume you're talking about your ex?"

"I'd rather not talk about him at all," she said, the slightest quiver in her neutral tone belying her control.

"Reid said the guy was an uptight prick."

"Reid says a lot of things he shouldn't." She shook her head. "I won't discuss this with you."

"Might help to get it off your chest."

Poor choice of cliché as his gaze strayed there and bam! The nipple pasties were front and foremost in his mind again.

"Reid was right." She sighed, a wistful sound that reached deep into his chest and tweaked at his hardened heart. "Uptight prick sums up Max nicely. Along with mid-life-crisis, philandering bastard."

Jack's hands curled into fists. "He cheated on you?"

She nodded, the wobble of her bottom lip reaching out to him like nothing else could. If she cried again, he was toast.

"We're done and I'm glad." She sucked in a deep breath. "So, where were we? That's right, you heading back to Sydney."

Grateful for the change of topic so he could regain control of the irrational rage coursing through his body at the thought of any asshole being dumb enough to cheat on Jess, he leaned back in the armchair and draped an arm across the back of it.

"I'm not leaving."

Her chin tilted up. "Neither am I."

"Hundred bucks says you can't last an hour working alongside me."

"A thousand says you won't last a day." She thrust out her chest for emphasis.

Damn, she didn't play fair.

"Low blow, Jess." He shifted in his seat. "You can't go using your sexiness as a weapon."

Her eyes widened and her delectable lips parted a fraction. "You think I'm sexy?"

If he hadn't heard her tentativeness with his own ears he wouldn't have believed it. For all her bluster and teasing earlier, she sounded exactly like she had a decade earlier: unsure, hesitant, innocent.

"Hell, you want me to make a damn list?" His gaze roamed her body and he wrenched it back to her face with effort.

"Please."

How could one whispered word slug him harder than a knockout punch he'd sustained in his last foster home before he'd run away to the outback?

He shook his head. "I can't play this game with you."

"Why not?" She deliberately focused on his lips, licked hers.

"Because I'm not a dumbass twenty any more and you're no longer a naïve eighteen."

Rather than backing down as he expected, she did the one thing guaranteed to make his libido sit up and howl.

She placed her hand on the top of his thigh, one inch shy of his crotch.

"Don't sweat it. I'll have a week on the island to change your mind."

"What frigging island?"

Her teasing, sweet smile filled him with dread. "Didn't

you know? Dorian's flying us to the wedding venue, his private island in the Caribbean, so we can finalize details."

"No way."

Fire sparked her eyes to caramel. "Fine. If you're not up to the challenge..."

Her fingertips edged closer to detonation zone and he leaped to his feet.

"Dorian and Zazz are counting on us." Her smug smile as her gaze zeroed in on his hard-on made him want to haul her over his knees and spank her. Hard. "You can't say no."

His cock twitched in agreement.

He was so screwed.

BUY NOW to keep reading...

After BRASH, check out Jess's brother Reid's story in BLUSH

Laying it all on the line for love...

Adele Radcliff has worked hard to erase the sins of her past. The ex-burlesque dancer is now an accountant in Vegas and has her life on track. Until one steamy interlude with her friend's brother changes everything...

Reid Harper may be tired of the hand-shaking, back-slapping and baby-kissing, but politics is all he knows. His job consumes him. Until he meets Adele and the gorgeous redhead becomes his new focus.

Reid wants a relationship, Adele doesn't. A decision reinforced when Adele discovers she's pregnant. She has too many secrets to hide and can't risk Reid getting too close.

But Reid has other ideas and when he learns the startling truth, how far will he go to prove their future is more important than the past?

ABOUT THE AUTHOR

USA TODAY bestselling and multi-award winning author Nicola Marsh writes page-turning fiction to keep you up all night.
She's published 77 books and sold 8 million copies worldwide.
She currently writes contemporary romance for Penguin Random House USA Berkley imprint, domestic suspense for Hachette UK's Bookouture imprint, and rural romance for Harper Collins Australia's Mira imprint.
She's also a Waldenbooks, Bookscan, Amazon, iBooks and Barnes & Noble bestseller, a RBY (Romantic Book of the Year) and National Readers' Choice Award winner, and a multi-finalist for a number of awards including the Romantic Times Reviewers' Choice Award, HOLT Medallion, Booksellers' Best, Golden Quill, Laurel Wreath, and More than Magic.
A physiotherapist for thirteen years, she now adores writing full time, raising her two dashing young heroes, sharing fine food with family and friends, and her favorite, curling up with a good book!

Printed in Great Britain
by Amazon